Beyond Good Friday

Jaison Ndlovu

Published by Jaison Ndlovu, 2024.

BEYOND GOOD FRIDAY

First edition. October 6, 2024.

ISBN: 979-8227527844

Written by Jaison Ndlovu.

Table of Contents

To my daughter, Lomalinda Grannie Ndhlovu, whose inspiring idea ignited this journey. To my sons Logic Amos, Eureka Eulogy, Russell Hillary and Elisha Heritage, not forgeting their sister, Misery, whose unwavering support and material assistance fueled its progression. To my spouse, Susan Ndlovu (nee Mahogo), whose genuine interest provided constant motivation. And to my dear mother, Resiya Magundwane, (nee Chikwinya), whose prayers guided every word written. To my grandchildren who I have always wanted to know and tell when I am gone. Last but not least, all my relatives. This book is a testament to the love, encouragement, and unity that has always surrounded me.

CHAPTER one

A Deeper Understanding of Passover and Easter

When we affirm the Bible as the true word of God, we must also uphold truthfulness in our understanding and application. Interestingly, the Bible refers to days of the week by their numerical sequence, rather than assigning specific names.

For instance, in Genesis 1:5 and Exodus 20:8-11, days are identified by their numerical order. However, humans have assigned names to days, derived from ancient pagan cultures and celestial bodies.

Notably, the seventh day, observed as the Sabbath, is not inherently a day's name. Instead, Sabbath denotes the act of rest, occurring on the seventh day.

The Bible's emphasis on numerical sequence underscores God's design for humanity to count and observe time, as seen in Genesis 1:14 and Exodus 16:4-5. Assigning names to days can be seen as a subtle rebellion against God's intention.

This divergence from biblical simplicity raises important questions. How do our cultural traditions align with biblical teachings? Do our naming conventions reflect our worship and values? What does this say about our relationship with the Lord worshipped by Jews and Gentiles?

By recognizing this disparity, we are reminded of the importance of returning to biblical foundations and embracing the simplicity of God's design. The Bible's silence on naming days suggests a focus on numerical sequence, highlighting God's sovereignty over time.

In this context, our understanding of time and worship is invited to align more closely with biblical principles, rather than cultural or pagan influences.

As we embark on our wayward examinations of Easter traditions, we'll commence with the inaugural day of this holiday, Good Friday, and uncover its significance. Assuming the Bible's accuracy, we'll delve into the underlying motives behind Good Friday's observance, questioning whether its origins are rooted in truth or misconception.

Is Good Friday genuinely "good," or does its significance stem from a misguided narrative? To answer this, we'll examine the biblical account of Jesus' crucifixion and resurrection, investigate the historical and cultural context surrounding Good Friday's establishment, and analyze potential motives behind its observance, exploring whether they align with biblical teachings.

By scrutinizing the facts and motivations, we aim to separate truth from tradition, gaining a deeper understanding of Good Friday's authenticity and significance within the Christian faith.

We'll reference key scriptures, such as Matthew 27:32-56, which describes Jesus' crucifixion, John 19:31-37, which recounts Jesus' burial, and 1 Corinthians 15:3-4, which affirms Jesus' resurrection.

Through this inquiry, our goal is to uncover the biblical basis for Good Friday's observance, identify potential discrepancies between scripture and tradition, and clarify the meaning and significance of Good Friday for believers today.

Observed on the Friday before Easter Sunday, the day holds profound significance in the Christian calendar. It marks the solemn commemoration of Jesus Christ's crucifixion and ultimate sacrifice on the cross for the redemption of humanity. This day is reserved for introspection, fervent prayer, and reverence, as Christians worldwide unite in remembrance.

However, it is essential to acknowledge that the traditional observance of Good Friday is not entirely aligned with biblical accuracy. The term "Good Friday" is derived from the Old English phrase "God's Friday," signifying a day dedicated to God. The assumption that Friday was the day of crucifixion stems from the misconception that the day following was a Sabbath, without recognizing that biblical Sabbaths include Holy Convocation days, also known as High-day Sabbaths, not just the seventh day of the week.

This clarification invites a deeper understanding of the biblical narrative, encouraging a more nuanced appreciation for the events surrounding Jesus' crucifixion and resurrection.

In ancient times, the concept of the Sabbath held a nuanced understanding. The people of that era recognized the Sabbath as a distinct day, separate from other days of rest or observance, but not limited to only the seventh day. This understanding is crucial to grasp, as it underscores the significance of the

Sabbath in the biblical narrative, even though the Seventh Day was the regular Sabbath.

Before we proceed, let's distinguish between Passover and Easter, and explore which feast influenced the other.

Passover is a significant Jewish holiday that commemorates the Israelites' liberation from slavery in Egypt, as told in the book of Exodus. It is observed on the 14th day of the Hebrew month of Abib/Nisan, typically in March or April. Easter, on the other hand, is a Christian holiday that celebrates the resurrection of Jesus Christ. It is observed on a Sunday, typically in March or April, and is linked to the Passover because Jesus' crucifixion and resurrection occurred during the Passover festival.

While Passover and Easter are distinct holidays, they share a historical connection. Jesus' Last Supper with his disciples was a Passover Seder, and his crucifixion and resurrection are seen by Christians as the fulfillment of the Passover themes of redemption and liberation.

Over time, Easter has incorporated distinctive traditions and symbolism, such as Easter eggs, originating from ancient pagan cultures (e.g., Germanic and Anglo-Saxon). Nevertheless, Easter's roots are intertwined with the Jewish Passover observance (Exodus 12:1-28). However, not everyone embraces Easter eggs and associated customs. Many Christians strictly focus on commemorating Jesus Christ's death and resurrection (1 Corinthians 15:1-4), avoiding pagan influences.

The origin of the name "Easter" is complex and debated among scholars. The name may come from the Germanic goddess of spring and fertility, Eostre, whose festival was celebrated at the same time of year as the Christian holiday, and the name may have been adopted as a result of cultural syncretism.

Alternatively, the name "Easter" may come from the Hebrew word "Pesach" (Passover) or the Aramaic word "Pascha", which was used to describe the Jewish holiday. Early Christians may have adapted this name to create "Easter".

The exact timing of when the name "Easter" originated is unclear, but it is believed to have emerged in the early Middle Ages, around the 6th or 7th century CE. The name "Easter" was first used in English in the 7th century, and it gradually replaced earlier names for the holiday, such as "Pascha" or "Resurrection Day".

However, the name "Easter" is not universally used.

Fundamentally, is Easter synonymous with the Passover holy days? While spiritual significance takes precedence over physical alignment in the church, our physical reality remains integral to our lives. Literal events and dates hold importance. Good Friday, observed on the Friday preceding Easter Sunday, commemorates Jesus Christ's crucifixion and redemption of humanity (1 Corinthians 5:7-8). This solemn day is reserved for introspection, prayer, and reverence. However, the question persists: is it truly Passover, or a distinct celebration?

For clarity, let's examine the pivotal Council of Nicaea (325 AD), where church fathers collectively established Easter, diverging from the biblical Passover. At this council, they ignored specific dates and instead adopted a weekly observance, fixing Easter on the first day of the week, presumed to be the Resurrection Day. We will revisit this topic to explore whether Jesus Christ actually rose on Sunday or shortly before.

The Council brought together Christian bishops from the Eastern and Western Roman Empires. Emperor Constantine I, who ruled from 306 to 337 AD, convened and presided over the council. Other key figures included Alexander of Alexandria, Bishop of Alexandria from 312 to 328 AD, who played a crucial role in shaping the council's agenda. Athanasius of Alexandria, Alexander's protégé and future bishop, also attended. Eusebius of Nicomedia, Bishop of Nicomedia from 318 to 341 AD, led the Arian faction, while Marcellus of Ancyra, Bishop of Ancyra from 314 to 336 AD, strongly opposed Arianism. Approximately 300 bishops represented various regions.

The Council of Nicaea resolved several significant issues that continue to impact Christianity and Western society today. One key issue addressed was the controversy surrounding the day of Easter (Pascha). The council decreed that Easter would be celebrated on the first Sunday following the full moon after the vernal equinox, effectively separating it from the Jewish Passover. This was a set day, unlike the Passover's set date.

Although Good Friday was not explicitly mentioned at the Nicaea Council, the separation of Easter from the Jewish Passover likely influenced Western Christianity's observation of a "Day of Preparation" or "Parasceve" on Friday during the 4th to 6th centuries. By the 7th to 8th centuries, Good Friday had emerged as a distinct observance linked to Easter. During the Medieval period, Good Friday evolved into a day of solemn procession, prayer, and cross veneration.

In this context, Easter and Good Friday appear to have developed into separate observances, losing their original ties to Passover which is observed on specific dates of the Hebrew calendar, the 14th to 21st Abib. Good Friday has arguably become a commemorative day, analogous to internationally recognized days like Mother's Day, Father's Day, or International Women's Day. Such days function as tributes, disconnected from their historical roots.

In contrast, Passover remains an observance deeply rooted in its original significance and timing, commemorating the Israelites' liberation from slavery in Egypt. For Christians, the Paschal period – from Jesus' crucifixion to His resurrection – coincides with the Jewish Passover.

Some Christians choose to observe Passover according to the Jewish calendar, aligning with the biblical account in Exodus 12.

Interestingly, Easter days are determined by lunar calculations. By embracing lunar dictates, Christianity honors its Jewish roots while celebrating the resurrection of Jesus Christ. Consequently, Easter's date varies annually, falling between March 22 and April 25.

The celestial bodies in the sky, the lunar included, serve a purpose, not mere decoration. They are useful, even essential, to humanity. For example, the magi from the East followed a star to locate Jesus' birthplace, demonstrating their significance.

The Bible cautions against astrology, not because it's inherently evil, but because its power demands responsible handling. Without proper understanding, astrology can be detrimental.

According to Deuteronomy 29:29, God's revelations are meant for us and our children, while secrets, including astrology and occult mysteries, remain under the Lord's discretion. This scripture cautions us to prioritize revealed truths and avoid speculative or occult pursuits (Colossians 2:8, 1 Timothy 6:20-21). Consequently, obediently following God's commands is the safest approach.

Consider radio waves, which traverse vacuums and influence human life. Before their discovery, who knew they existed? Similarly, the zodiac impacts individuals from birth, making timing crucial. Therefore, the best approach is to follow God's orders obediently, as safety precautions.

God's prohibition on certain practices (Deuteronomy 29:29) acknowledges their existence and potency, but reserves them for His divine purposes, not human execution. Astronomers' emphasis on precise timing underscores the intricate design of God's celestial workings, demonstrating His sovereignty over all.

And so, observing feasts like Passover on precise dates and days synchronizes us with the Divine and natural rhythms. Random timing won't suffice; calibration with the cosmic entity is essential.

The Council of Nicaea's decision to fix Easter Sunday on the first Sunday after the full moon following the vernal equinox seems perplexing, given the historical context. However, a plausible explanation lies in the variable date of 14 Abib. The lunar-based Hebrew calendar meant the date wouldn't always fall on the day of the week, in this case Wednesday, as we shall see later. Consequently, Jesus' resurrection, occurring on Sunday dawn, wouldn't consistently align with the calendar. For this reason, the Council sought stability and uniformity.

While their decision was practical, adopting the name "Easter" for the for the "Passion Week" creates confusion, as it overlaps with pre-Christian, pagan spring festivals (Eostre/Ostara). The name obliterates the historical connection to Passover and Jesus' crucifixion.

The Christian celebration of Easter has a complex history, raising questions about its alignment with the faith's core values. While early Christianity sought to capitalize on existing gatherings and festivals, integrating pagan traditions into the resurrection narrative sparks debate.

As mentioned earlier, the term 'Easter' possibly originated from Eostre, the ancient Germanic goddess of spring and fertility. Her spring equinox festival was likely absorbed into Christianity, incorporating symbols such as eggs (representing new life) and rabbits (embodying fertility).

While the Council of Nicaea in 325 AD formally established Easter as a Christian holiday. Over time, Easter evolved, blending Jewish and pagan elements with Christian traditions.

This blending of traditions raises concerns. Is it viable to capitalize on pagan Easter celebrations and turn them into a Christian gathering? By retaining Eostre's name and symbols, are Christians inadvertently venerating the ancient goddess?

This practice seems to diverge from the Christian faith, where Jesus Christ is the center of everything. The presence of pagan elements may shift focus away from Jesus and onto worldly themes.

Scripture warns against such syncretism, urging separation from worldly influences and avoidance of idolatry. In Exodus 20:3-5, God commands, "You shall have no other gods before Me." Revelation 18:4 cautions, "Come out of her, my people, lest you share in her sins."

The implications are significant. By blending pagan practices with Christian worship, the gospel may be diluted, and confusion may arise.

However, viewed from a different perspective, Christians commemorate Jesus' Resurrection (1 Corinthians 15:1-4), rather than celebrating Easter gods. This distinction highlights the centrality of Jesus' victory over death in Christian faith. Interestingly, our days of the week have origins worth noting. Sunday, for instance, comes from "dies Solis," honoring the Sun god. We have "Sunday School," yet those attending church on Saturday call it "Sabbath School." However, when asked which day is the Sabbath, they'll say Saturday, named after Saturn.

They can't simply say the Seventh Day because its identification depends on the starting point. In Zimbabwe, the Ndebele and Shona tribes count Monday as the First Day, Tuesday as the second, and so on, making Friday the fifth day and implying Sunday is the seventh.

Consider the name "Baal", which carries multiple nuanced meanings: father, lord, and husband. In biblical contexts, "Baal" refers to two distinct concepts. On one hand, it designates the pagan god Baal, worshipped by ancient Israel's neighbors and, occasionally, by the Israelites themselves (Numbers 25:3; 1 Kings 17:1). On the other hand, "Baal" can serve as a title or term for God, emphasizing His lordship or ownership, as seen in Hosea 2:16.

Although Baal is notoriously associated with pagan worship in the stories of Elijah and Jezebel, Scripture reveals a nuanced perspective. In Hosea 2:16, God surprisingly acknowledges "Baal" as one of His own names, highlighting its original Hebrew meaning, "Lord" or "Husband." Similarly, calling the Resurrection Day "Easter" – originally a spring festival honoring a pagan goddess – doesn't necessarily imply idolatrous intent. Many innocently use the term, unaware of its origins, having effectively repurposed it to celebrate Christ's resurrection.

Interestingly, the Bible refers to three Hebrew youths as Shadrach, Meshach, and Abednego, names given to them by the Babylonian king Nebuchadnezzar in honor of his gods. Their original Hebrew names were Hananiah, Mishael, and Azariah, but Scripture adopts the pagan-derived names. This precedent shows that using names with non-divine origins isn't unprecedented. Similarly, calling the Resurrection Day "Easter," a term rooted in ancient pagan celebrations, doesn't necessarily detract from its Christian significance.

In God's sovereign plan, every event has a purpose and nothing occurs by chance. Even seemingly accidental discoveries, like penicillin and X-rays, are part of His intricate design. God is not capricious or playful; everything serves a greater good.

The biblical account of Aaron's rod transforming into a snake before Pharaoh illustrates this principle (Exodus 7:8-12). This miraculous event foreshadowed Jesus Christ's power working through His invisible church. Aaron's rod, empowered by God, swallowed the counterfeit snakes produced by Pharaoh's wise men and sorcerers, symbolizing the showdown by Christ against all sin and death. Aaron's snake swallowed the evil snakes. Here, Aaron's snake represented righteousness, and the other snakes symbolized the evil. Aaron's snake devoured all evil snakes. In it was the DNA of every evil force, and like a vaccinated body, all evil cannot cause him harm.

Similarly, the Bronze Serpent, described in Numbers 21:4-9 and 2 Kings 18:4, presents an intriguing paradox. Initially, a symbol of pagan fertility cults and later associated with the devil from Genesis to Revelation, its use was commanded by God Himself. This unexpected appropriation would have been unthinkable to Jewish people and Christians if not ordained by God.

Interestingly, Jesus Christ drew a profound parallel between the Bronze Serpent and His own crucifixion. Just as Moses lifted the serpent on a pole, bringing healing to the Israelites, Jesus declared that He, the Son of Man, would be lifted up on the Cross, bringing salvation to humanity (John 3:14-15).

This striking analogy highlights God's ability to redeem and transform even the most unlikely symbols, imbuing them with new, redemptive meaning.

Another example is the modern celebration of Christmas which began taking shape in the 4th century. Although its early history is scarce, here's a concise overview:

In 336 AD, Roman Emperor Constantine, a Christian, designated December 25 as Jesus' birthday. Pope Julius I officially solidified this date in 350 AD. As Christmas spread throughout Europe in the 5th-6th centuries, local traditions and customs were incorporated.

Interestingly, the Julian calendar, used at that time, influenced the interpretation of biblical months. The "twelfth month" mentioned in Scripture corresponded to December, rather than the Hebrew month of Adar.

This date coincided with an existing festival, originating from the Babylonian exile. On the 25th day of the twelfth month, gifts were exchanged, reminiscent of the festivities when Jehoiachin, the king of Judah, was released (Jeremiah 52:31-34). Whether rooted in fact or legend, this day was transformed into a Christian holiday.

Today, Christmas combines festivities with solemn praise and worship services, commemorating Jesus' birth. This transformation illustrates how ancient Jewish and pagan feasts, names, and events were repurposed for God's service.

These instances demonstrate God's ability to reclaim and transform cultural practices, imbuing them with new, redemptive meaning.

Indeed, it's a beautiful manifestation of God's transformative power, where former instruments of conflict are repurposed for noble ends. Just as the prophet Isaiah envisioned (Isaiah 2:4), swords are beaten into ploughshares and knives into pruning hooks, symbols of warfare transformed into tools for cultivation and growth.

Similarly, God redeems cultural practices, names, and symbols, once rooted in paganism, for His glorious purposes. This redemption reflects His ability to restore and reclaim all things, making the ordinary, extraordinary, and the profane, sacred.

Additionally, Sunday, a day once dedicated to pagan solar deities, was redeemed by Christ's resurrection, becoming the Lord's Day – a global celebration of hope, renewal, and worship. This profound transformation exemplifies God's power to reclaim and redefine cultural practices, turning even the most unlikely symbols into testaments of His glory.

In this context, despite its origins, the Easter holiday is not inherently pagan. Similarly, the cross, once a symbol of execution and shame (Galatians 3:13, Deuteronomy 21:23), has been transformed into a powerful emblem of hope, love, and faith. Although the cross was initially detested by the Jews as an instrument of death, Jesus' sacrifice upon it redeemed its meaning. Now, the cross is universally recognized as a symbol of salvation, transcending its former negativity to become an enduring beacon of hope (Romans 5:8).

The cross now conveys a life-giving message, which may seem foolish to those who are perishing, but to us who believe, it embodies the power of God (1 Corinthians 1:18). As the most universally recognized and revered symbol in human history, the cross transcends language and culture, communicating hope, redemption, and salvation to all. Through the cross, Jesus' sacrifice continues to inspire faith, comfort the afflicted, and transform lives forever.

Despite Good Friday not specifically commemorating the crucifixion day and Easter's pagan origins, these observances stem from the Jewish Passover. Their significance transcends names and symbols, focusing on the essence: honoring God's redemption.

Names and symbols are mere vessels; what matters is the heart and intention behind them – worshiping the one true God or idolatrous gods.

In conclusion, Passover remains deeply rooted in its original significance and timing, commemorating the Israelites' liberation from Egyptian slavery. For Christians, Easter – the Paschal period from Jesus' crucifixion to His resurrection – coincides with Jewish Passover but holds a distinct significance. Easter commemorates Jesus Christ's crucifixion and resurrection, unrelated to the Israelites' physical liberation from Egyptian slavery.

Instead, the Israelites' liberation foreshadowed humanity's liberation from Satan's bondage. At the core of Easter is Jesus Christ's resurrection, marking the successful establishment of His invisible church.

And so, let's explore the rich history and spiritual significance of Passover, the Sabbath, and other holy days, tracing their origins and uncovering the depth of God's redemptive plan.

CHAPTER Two

Beyond Good Friday

Let's revisit Good Friday. As previously discussed, this day was referred to as the Sixth Day of the week. Notably, the Bible doesn't use alphabetical names for the days, instead identifying them by their numerical sequence, from one to seven, with the Seventh Day designated as the Sabbath. This numerical naming convention provides a unique perspective on the ancient Jewish calendar and its significance in understanding the biblical narrative.

The term "Sabbath" referred to the significance of the seventh day, determined by counting, as well as any other day designated as such by divine appointment. Initially, elsewhere and in Egypt, before the official establishment of the nation of Israel on 1 Abib/Nissan, only the regular seventh-day of the week may have been recognized as a Sabbath, based on the biblical context. However, during the first month of the new Jewish calendar year, as proclaimed by God to Moses while still in Egypt, Abib had two additional special Sabbaths, known as High Day Sabbaths. These High Day Sabbaths either coincided with the regular Sabbaths on the 15th and 21st of Abib in the first year or stood alone from the regular Sabbaths. In subsequent years, some years had more than five Sabbaths in the month of Abib, comprising four regular Sabbaths and two High Day Sabbaths.

Furthermore, the Bible does not explicitly state that the two Sabbaths mentioned were the first Sabbaths observed since creation. Additionally, it is unclear whether the seventh day of the week was originally referred to as the Sabbath or simply the day when God, not humanity, rested.

Moreover, the biblical account of creation (Genesis 2:2-3) does not explicitly link the seventh day with the term 'Sabbath.' It was only later, through the Ten Commandments (Exodus 20:8-11), that the Sabbath was formally instituted as a day of rest for humanity. We will explore this further in due course.

The traditional observance of Good Friday as the day of Jesus Christ's crucifixion is deeply ingrained in Christian tradition, despite alternative scholarly interpretations suggesting a different timeline. A closer examination of the Gospels, particularly in the context of Jewish festivals, reveals that there may have been two Sabbaths during the week of Jesus' crucifixion. The "High Sabbath" refers to the first day of the Feast of Unleavened Bread, which could fall on any day of the week, in addition to the regular weekly Sabbath (Saturday).

While Good Friday remains the traditional day of observance, its origins date back to the early Christian church and have been maintained for centuries, becoming an integral part of Christian liturgy and culture. The sequence of Holy Week events provides a coherent and meaningful framework for Christians to remember and celebrate the Passion, Death, and Resurrection of Jesus. However, it's important to acknowledge that the majority interpretation may not always be correct, as seen in the example of the twelve spies sent to view Canaan, where only Joshua and Caleb brought back accurate reports.

Scholarly debates and interpretations continue to explore the historical and biblical details of these events. Nevertheless, for many Christians, the significance of Jesus' sacrifice and resurrection takes precedence over the exact chronology. Yet, as part of our purpose on earth, we strive to attain knowledge of the truth, which includes knowing Christ and understanding God's revelations, as stated in Deuteronomy 29:29. This pursuit of truth ultimately sets us free.

The Israelites' counting from 1 Abib, separating a lamb on the 10th day, and keeping it until the 14th of Abib was no coincidence, but rather a deliberate design by God. This precise counting and adherence to God's directives underscore the importance of exactness in following His commands. The subsequent instructions to observe special Sabbaths on the 15th and 21st of Abib further emphasize the significance of precise timing in God's plan.

The notion that the significance of Jesus' sacrifice and resurrection supersedes the exact chronology may be seen as a human excuse for disobedience or inattention to detail. The fact that Jesus Christ died on the exact day of the Passover lamb, a tradition rooted in the Hebrew calendar, is not mere coincidence. Rather, it highlights the intricate connection between the Old and New Testaments, demonstrating God's masterful plan and attention to detail.

Jesus' crucifixion on the day of the Passover lamb holds profound significance, as it fulfills the prophetic symbolism of the lamb as a sacrifice for sin. This precise timing underscores the importance of understanding and adhering to God's chronological plan, rather than dismissing it as inconsequential. By examining the exact chronology of events, we can gain a deeper appreciation for the intricate tapestry of God's plan and the significance of Jesus' sacrifice and resurrection.

Moreover, if God provided Noah with precise measurements, specific types of timber, and exact numbers of animals to include in the Ark, demonstrating attention to detail in His instructions, why do some theologians and scholars downplay the importance of exact chronology in understanding Jesus' sacrifice and resurrection? Do they not recognize that every detail, including timing, works together to fulfill God's glorious purpose and will?

The precision in God's instructions to Noah underscores the significance of exactness in carrying out His plans. Similarly, the exact timing of Jesus' crucifixion and resurrection, coinciding with the Hebrew calendar and fulfilling Old Testament prophecies, demonstrates the intricate harmony of God's plan.

Furthermore, as believers, we are called to judge angels and rule with Jesus Christ in the future. To do so, we must adhere to the precise layout and parameters set by God, rather than relying on assumptions or vague interpretations. Ruling according to God's exact plan requires understanding and respecting the chronology of events, just as Noah followed God's exact instructions to build the Ark.

By acknowledging the importance of exact chronology, we can gain a deeper understanding of God's masterful plan, appreciate the intricate connections between Old and New Testaments, and prepare ourselves for our future roles in judging and ruling according to His will.

It's better to attempt and fail than to fail to try altogether. Simply accepting Good Friday without questioning its accuracy, despite evidence suggesting it's incorrect, makes us disobedient and dishonest - willful sinners. If Jesus himself declared that, like Jonah, he would spend three days and three nights in the heart of the earth, who are we to limit his time in the grave to just one day and two nights, from Friday evening to Sunday morning?

Jesus' specific statement of three days and three nights must hold significance, or he wouldn't have emphasized it. By ignoring or downplaying this detail, we risk diminishing the importance of his words and the significance of his sacrifice. Let us strive to understand and honor the precise timing of Jesus' crucifixion, burial, and resurrection, rather than settling for a potentially flawed tradition.

If the chronological sequence is insignificant, why did God instruct the Israelites to count the days to determine the Sabbath? Why the establishment of a calendar and a clock? Just as science relies heavily on mathematics and chronology to understand the world, shouldn't we expect even greater precision when it comes to the things of the Lord?

In other words, if precision and timing are crucial in scientific pursuits, shouldn't they be even more vital in understanding and honoring God's plans and purposes? The fact that God emphasized the importance of counting, calendars, and timing in His instructions suggests that chronological sequence indeed matters, and we should strive to understand and respect His precise timing.

In the context of chronological timing, farmers can deliberately create a controlled or planned breeding period for their cattle to optimize milk production for calves and consumption. This approach ensures that most calves are born within a specific period, typically during the wet season when pasture is abundant, allowing for optimal nutrition. By timing calving to coincide with peak pasture growth, farmers can ensure that lactating cows receive adequate nutrition.

Breeding cows during a specific period increases the chances of having more cows in milk simultaneously, resulting in a surplus for consumption. Controlled breeding enables farmers to plan and manage their herd more effectively, including scheduling vaccinations, nutrition, and parasite control. Techniques such as artificial insemination, natural breeding with selected bulls, hormonal synchronization, and management of bull exposure can be employed to achieve this. By optimizing their cattle's breeding and milk production through controlled breeding programs, farmers can ultimately improve their livelihoods and food security, all of which relies on precise chronological timing for best results.

The significance of timing is evident in various aspects of life, from the celestial to the mundane. The magi's recognition of Jesus Christ's birth, as signaled by the star, underscores the importance of timing in understanding divine events. It was no accident that Jesus was born on a specific day, as this timing aligns with prophetic fulfillments and God's master plan.

Similarly, civil authorities require the exact date and place of birth on a child's birth certificate to establish a precise record of identity and chronology. This information is crucial for legal, social, and administrative purposes, highlighting the importance of timing in human affairs.

In nature, trees exhibit annual rings on their trunks, which determine their age and provide a chronological record of growth. This phenomenon demonstrates that chronology is an inherent aspect of life, even in the natural world.

The concept of age relies on chronology, as it measures the duration between birth and the present moment. Without chronology, age would be meaningless, and predicting the remaining time without knowing the starting time would be impossible.

Furthermore, timing plays a critical role in various fields, including astronomy, where planetary alignments and celestial events are precisely timed. In history, timing is essential for understanding cause-and-effect relationships and contextualizing events. In science, measuring intervals, frequencies, and rates of change relies heavily on accurate timing. In medicine, timing is crucial for diagnosing and treating patients, as well as understanding disease progression. Additionally, in finance, timing is vital for managing investments, predicting market trends, and setting deadlines. These examples illustrate the pervasive importance of timing in diverse aspects of life, highlighting its significance in understanding and navigating complex phenomena.

And so, timing is essential for understanding and navigating various aspects of life, from divine events to natural phenomena and human affairs. Its significance cannot be overstated, as it provides context, meaning, and structure to our experiences. In this context, the idea that the importance of Jesus' sacrifice and resurrection eclipses the need for precise chronology may be viewed as a convenient justification for neglecting or disregarding the specifics of God's plan. By downplaying the significance of exact timing, individuals may be excusing themselves from the responsibility of carefully examining and adhering to the divine schedule, ultimately revealing a lack of attention to detail or even disobedience.

The revelation that Jesus Christ's birth likely occurred around 6 BC, rather than AD 1 as calculated by Dionysius Exiguus, was a significant discovery made by later historians and scholars through careful examination of various indicators and abundant knowledge. However, despite this finding, the calendar system established by Dionysius Exiguus has been retained to avoid confusion and ensure continuity. Altering the calendar to align with the more accurate historical estimate of Jesus' birth would have caused substantial disruption, as the Anno Domini (AD) system had become deeply ingrained in European and global societies, forming the basis of the widely used Gregorian calendar.

Adjusting the starting point of the calendar would have required a monumental task of recalibrating all historical dates, rendering it highly impractical. Consequently, the original calculation by Dionysius Exiguus remains in use, prioritizing consistency and practicality over historical accuracy. This raises important questions: Is this not a form of deception? Is it not a deliberate choice to ignore the truth and disobey the principles of accuracy? Does it not align with the scripture that declares, "To him who knows what is right and does not do it, to him it is sin" (James 4:17)?

By maintaining the Dionysius Exiguus calculation, are we not perpetuating a historical inaccuracy, and in doing so, are we not compromising our commitment to truth and obedience to God's principles? This conundrum highlights the tension between practicality and accuracy, raising important questions about the importance of truth and obedience in our lives.

A pregnant woman eagerly anticipates the arrival of her child, and her excitement is heightened by knowing the expected due date. However, this anticipation relies on her understanding of the gestation period and the conception date. Without this knowledge, predicting the birth date would be impossible. Similarly, horoscopes, which are based on the positions of celestial bodies at the exact time and place of an individual's birth, require precise chronological information to generate accurate readings.

As previously mentioned, the Bible explicitly warns against practicing astrology and divination, as seen in Deuteronomy 18:10-12 and Isaiah 47:13-14. The fact that the Bible prohibits these practices implies that they have some basis in reality, as it would not condemn unrealistic or ineffective phenomena. This suggests that chronological dates, including the time and place of birth, hold significance in understanding human affairs and destinies.

Moreover, the importance of chronological dates extends beyond horoscopes and birth predictions. In various aspects of life, precise timing and scheduling are crucial, from medical procedures to financial transactions, and historical record-keeping. The significance of chronological dates underscores the interconnectedness of time, events, and human experiences.

By recognizing the importance of chronological dates, we acknowledge the intricate web of relationships between celestial bodies, human affairs, and the passage of time. This understanding encourages us to approach life with a deeper appreciation for the complexities and mysteries that surround us.

The seventh day of the week holds a unique significance, designated as the regular Sabbath, a day of rest and rejuvenation. The deliberate act of numbering the days, rather than naming them, was a divine decision made by God Himself. This emphasis on numbering highlights the importance of chronological timing in understanding the Sabbath's significance.

On the first day of creation, God established the concept of day and night by creating light, setting the precedent for the subsequent six days. Each day was a repetition of the first, underscoring the idea that the day is a singular entity, recurring in an ongoing cycle. When this cycle reaches its seventh iteration, it becomes the day of rest, the regular Sabbath.

The Sabbath's determination relies on precise counting, which is why it was not assigned a specific name. This method of calculation also explains why the Sabbath begins at different times for individuals in disparate locations, such as Australia and Los Angeles, USA. The distinction in time zones necessitates accurate chronological timing to ensure the correct observance of the Sabbath.

In this context, the importance of precise chronological timing becomes evident. It allows for the proper identification of the seventh day, enabling individuals to observe the Sabbath in harmony with God's original intent. By recognizing the significance of numbering and the recurring nature of the day, we can appreciate the intricate design of the weekly cycle and the special place of the Sabbath within it.

The Apostolic notion that all days are equally important stems from the understanding that the day is a singular, recurring entity, continuously cycling until God decrees its cessation. This perspective emphasizes the unity and interconnectedness of time, where each day is a repetition of the first, forming an unbroken cycle.

The seventh recurrence of this cycle marks the weekly Sabbath, a day of rest and rejuvenation. This repetitive pattern extends beyond the weekly cycle, forming months and years through the accumulation of these cycles. The lunar cycle, comprising approximately 29.5 days, gives rise to the month, while the solar cycle, consisting of approximately 365.24 days, yields the year.

The importance of chronology lies in its role as the foundation for this intricate system of timekeeping. By counting the number of repetitions, we can accurately determine the passage of time, ensuring the proper observance of sacred days, such as the weekly Sabbath, and the alignment of our lives with God's rhythms.

This understanding underscores the significance of chronology in various aspects of life, from the celestial mechanics governing the movements of planets and stars to the biological cycles governing human life. By recognizing the repetitive nature of time and the importance of counting, we can appreciate the harmony and order that pervade the universe, reflecting the wisdom and design of its Creator.

The fall of Jericho's walls, as narrated in the Book of Joshua (Joshua 6:20), unequivocally demonstrates divine intervention, showcasing supernatural forces beyond natural laws. However, the instructions followed by Joshua and the Israelites cannot be overlooked, as God's purposeful plans are never frivolous. From a physical science perspective, the Israelites' marching around Jericho (Joshua 6:1-27) defies natural explanations.

Considering the event's historical and spiritual significance, a hypothetical analysis from a physical science perspective offers intriguing possibilities. The synchronized marching of approximately 600,000 men, plus women and children (Numbers 1:46), could have generated low-frequency vibrations. Amplified by Jericho's geography and architecture, these vibrations might have resonated with the walls' natural frequency, causing structural instability.

Furthermore, the loud cry emitted by the Israelites on the seventh day, after marching around seven times, could have generated a sonic wave, potentially compromising the walls' structural integrity. This phenomenon is analogous to acoustic resonance, where sound waves can shatter or damage materials.

Similarly, as described in Joshua 6:1-27, the Israelites' uniform march around Jericho may have had a comparable effect to a glass cutter's scoring, which weakens glass without cutting it, rendering it susceptible to breakage.

Moreover, their marching may have "scored" the walls of Jericho, setting them up for catastrophic failure. Then, as mentioned earlier, the loud cry emitted by the Israelites on the seventh day, after marching around seven times, could have provided the external force needed to breach the weakened line, causing the walls to collapse. The combination of seismic resonance from the marching and the subsequent sonic wave from the Israelites' cry may have collectively contributed to the miraculous collapse of Jericho's walls.

While these hypotheses offer intriguing possibilities, it's essential to recognize that the events at Jericho were ultimately a miraculous demonstration of God's power and faithfulness to His people. Nevertheless, God's instructions to Joshua for a seven-day procession were deliberate and meaningful, underscoring the divine significance of this ritual.

Thus, adhering to God's precise timeline was vital for the miraculous outcome. The systematic marches and final loud cry had tangible physical effects on Jericho's walls, demonstrating the importance of timing in unlocking divine intervention. Deviating from this schedule could have resulted in failure or unintended consequences.

In this context, we cannot arbitrarily assign the crucifixion day to suit our convenience; we must adhere to historical accuracy.

The account of Jericho's wall collapse in Joshua 6 raises intriguing questions about the interplay between divine intervention and natural phenomena. While science remains uncertain about the exact cause of the walls' downfall, biblical context suggests God's actions were deliberate and purposeful.

Notably, God's instruction to march around Jericho for seven days (Joshua 6:3-4) was more than a random command. This seven-day period held significance, as it mirrored the creation week and highlighted God's sovereignty over time.

However, an examination of the Israelites' actions during this period reveals an interesting anomaly. For six days, they marched around the city once daily, but on the seventh day – typically considered the Sabbath – they marched around the city seven times before the walls collapsed (Joshua 6:15-16).

This detail implies that the Israelites did not observe a traditional Sabbath rest on the seventh day. Instead, they engaged in an intensified ritual, underscoring the uniqueness of this event.

This episode challenges traditional views on Sabbath observance, encouraging a nuanced understanding. The Sabbath, instituted later in Exodus 16 and Deuteronomy 5, served as a memorial to God's creation and deliverance.

The Jericho account in Joshua 6 demonstrates flexibility within biblical narratives, where divine commands take precedence over ritual norms. By examining this event, we gain valuable insights into God's sovereign control over time and events, as well as the intricate intersection of ritual and divine command.

Moreover, Joshua 6 highlights the complexities surrounding Sabbath observance in biblical narratives. This rich historical context invites deeper exploration of the biblical narrative, revealing the intricate relationships between faith, ritual, and divine intervention.

Through this lens, we see that biblical narratives often present multifaceted perspectives, inviting readers to consider the dynamic interplay between divine instruction, ritual practices, and historical context. This nuanced approach fosters a deeper appreciation for the biblical account, underscoring the significance of context and divine sovereignty.

Let's reconvene later to further explore this Sabbath topic.

CHAPTER three

The Quest for Accuracy

The Easter holiday, spanning from Good Friday to Easter Monday, is the longest holiday on contemporary Christian calendars. This four-day period comprises distinct days: Good Friday, Holy Saturday (also known as Black Saturday), Easter Sunday, and Easter Monday. While Easter Monday holds multifaceted significance, encompassing religious, historical, cultural, and personal aspects, its importance varies among Christians. Notably, Easter and Passover, although distinct celebrations, share a historical connection, with Easter's roots tracing back to Passover. We will explore this relationship in greater detail later in this discussion.

Good Friday, as observed in contemporary times, commemorates the crucifixion of Jesus Christ, an event that redeemed humanity from the devil's grasp, restoring our relationship with God. This pivotal act of sacrifice, spanning over 5,000 years since the Fall of Man, is deemed 'good' because it brought salvation, forgiveness, and reconciliation to humanity.

Although Friday has traditionally been associated with Jesus' crucifixion, it is unlikely to be the actual day, as previously discussed. To determine the precise day, we must first establish the year of the event. Scholars have debated the timing of the crucifixion, with some arguing for a date between 30-33 AD. This date must be consistent with the events of crucifixion week and align with the broader biblical narrative.

To determine the year of Jesus Christ's death, it is essential to establish his birth year, which in turn allows us to calculate his age at the commencement of his ministry and the duration of his ministry. This information is crucial for understanding the timeline of his life and mission.

Historical records and biblical accounts provide clues about Jesus' birth and ministry. The Gospel of Luke (3:23) states that Jesus was "about 30 years old" when he began his ministry, which lasted approximately three years. By knowing the birth year, we can calculate his age at the start of his ministry and estimate the duration of his ministry. Once we establish Jesus' birth year, we can calculate his age at the start of his ministry and the duration of his ministry, ultimately leading us to determine the year of his death. This chronological framework is vital for understanding the life and mission of Jesus Christ and its significance in human history.

To set the stage for our examination of the events surrounding Jesus Christ's birth, let's take a step back and explore the origins of the BC and AD dating system. This brief detour will help us appreciate the historical context in which these events unfolded.

Dionysius Exiguus, also known as Dionysius the Humble, was a 6th-century monk born around 470 AD in Scythia Minor, which is present-day Romania. He is best known for creating the Anno Domini (AD) dating system, which is used to number the years in the Gregorian and Julian calendars.

Dionysius was a highly respected scholar and theologian. He translated 401 church canons from Greek into Latin, including important decrees from early church councils. He also developed new Easter tables, which helped standardize the calculation of the date of Easter across the Christian world. His work had a lasting impact on both the church and the broader historical timeline, as the AD system became widely adopted and remains in use today.

Dionysius Exiguus introduced the Anno Domini (AD) system, creating a Christian calendar that counts years from Jesus Christ's birth, purportedly in 1 AD. However, his calculations may have relied on incomplete and inaccurate records, as we will discuss later. The AD system starts with 1 BC and 1 AD, with the year 1 AD beginning on January 1 and ending on December 31. Conversely, the BC era counts backwards from the day preceding the commencement of AD 1.

Later, the BCE/CE notation emerged as a neutral alternative, avoiding explicit reference to Jesus Christ. BCE and CE share the same timeline and year numbering as BC and AD but are more inclusive and neutral. The underlying dating system remains the same, with 1 BCE equivalent to 1 BC and 1 CE equivalent to 1 AD.

The change in notation is largely semantic, aiming to make the dating system more inclusive. The underlying structure remains unchanged, and the years and events unfold in the same sequence regardless of the notation used. This is reminiscent of Shakespeare's phrase, "A rose by any other name would smell as sweet," highlighting that the name or label doesn't change the inherent nature or characteristics of something.

Using biblical timelines, we can calculate Jesus' age at death. With his ministry starting at approximately 30 years old (Luke 3:23) and lasting about 3 years, Jesus would have been around 33 years old when he died. Consequently, if Jesus was indeed born in 1 AD/CE, his death would fall around 33 AD/CE, supporting Dionysius Exiguus' estimated dating.

According to the Hebrew calendar in 33 AD, Friday corresponded to 14 Abib/Nissan, and the Sabbath fell on 15 Abib (3793 AM), April 4, 33 CE. This supports the Good Friday account of Jesus' crucifixion. Nevertheless, doubts persist regarding the fulfillment of Jesus' prophecy of three days and three nights in the tomb. Did Jonah's experience in the fish's belly mirror this timeframe? To clarify, we must investigate the inaugural Passover, which prefigured Jesus' experience. Analyzing its chronology and symbolism may shed light on this pivotal question.

Approximately two weeks prior to the Israelites' departure from Egypt, God instructed Moses and Aaron to recalibrate their calendar. As recorded in Exodus 12:2, God declared, "This month shall be for you the beginning of months. It shall be the first month of the year for you." This directive effectively reset the Israelites' calendar, establishing Abib (Nisan) as the inaugural month.

This recalibration of the calendar held great significance, as it marked a new beginning for the Israelites and aligned their worship and festivals with God's redemption plan. By designating Abib (Nisan) as the first month, God established a sacred rhythm that would shape the Israelites' identity and faith.

This indicates a reset of their calendar system, starting with the month of Abib (Nisan).

To facilitate our discussion, we'll use modern weekday names to the days of the week, although anciently they were identified numerically (First Day to Seventh Day), as seen in Genesis 1-2.

The practice of naming and linking each day of the week to one of the seven known celestial bodies originated in ancient Mesopotamia around 2000 BCE. The Mesopotamians recognized seven visible celestial bodies: the Sun, Moon, Mars, Mercury, Jupiter, Venus, and Saturn. They named each day after one of these bodies, creating a seven-day week.

As the Roman Empire expanded, the Germanic and Norse peoples adapted these names to their own gods, resulting in the modern English names for the days of the week, which corresponded to the celestial bodies:

- dies Solis (Sunday) - named after the Sun god
- dies Lunae (Monday) - named after the Moon goddess
- dies Martis (Tuesday) - named after Mars, the god of war
- dies Mercurii (Wednesday) - named after Mercury, the messenger god
- dies Iovis (Thursday) - named after Jupiter, the king of the gods
- dies Veneris (Friday) - named after Venus, the goddess of love
- dies Saturni (Saturday) - named after Saturn, the god of agriculture

This process of the adaptation and renaming of the days of the week by the Roman Empire and its influence on various cultures and languages occurred over several centuries, roughly spanning from:

- 1st century BCE: The Roman Empire began to expand, adopting the Mesopotamian system of naming days after celestial bodies and associating them with their own gods.

- 1st-5th centuries CE: As the Roman Empire expanded, they introduced their system to the Germanic and Norse peoples, who adapted the names to their own gods.

- 5th-10th centuries CE: The Germanic and Norse peoples, such as the Anglo-Saxons and Vikings, continued to use and adapt the Roman system, resulting in the modern English names for the days of the week.

- 11th-15th centuries CE: The Norman Conquest of England in 1066 introduced French influences, which further solidified the modern English names for the days of the week.

So, the adaptation and renaming of the days of the week occurred over approximately 1,500 years, from the 1st century BCE to the 15th century CE. From this point on, we'll use Sunday (Day One), Monday (Day Two), Tuesday (Day Three), Wednesday (Day Four), Thursday (Day Five), Friday (Day Six), and Saturday (Day Seven).

For this discussion, and for pointers we'll address later, let's assume the initial Passover preparation day fell on Tuesday, beginning at sunset on Monday and ending at sunset on Tuesday. According to Jewish tradition, which aligns with the biblical norm established in Genesis 1:5 and Leviticus 23:32, the day begins at sunset. Therefore, Monday evening was already considered Tuesday, the third day of the week, 13 Abib/Nissan. This was the day of preparation, preceding what was later known as the Passover day.

On Tuesday evening, marking the start of the Jewish fourth day of the week, Wednesday, the 14th day of Abib began, which was Passover day. This day started at sunset on Tuesday evening. Later that night, the angel of the Lord struck down all the firstborn in Egypt, passing over the houses protected by the blood. As recorded in Exodus 12:13 and 23-27, the angel's act of passing over the Israelites' homes, sparing their firstborn, gave rise to the name 'Passover'.

From sunset on Wednesday to sunset on Thursday, it was the 15th day of Abib, the first day of Unleavened Bread and the first High Day Sabbath of the Feast of Unleavened Bread.

Thursday's sunset marked the beginning of Friday, the 16th day of Abib, a regular workday and the second day of the feast. The feast continued until the seventh day, the 21st of Abib, which was also a High Day Sabbath.

Notably, the period from the 15th of Abib (High Day Sabbath) to the 21st of Abib (High Day Sabbath) consisted of seven days, inclusive of both Sabbaths. This differs from the weekly Sabbath cycle (Saturday to Saturday), which encompasses eight days and implies an overlap into the next week. We will explore this further later.

For now, let's focus on the period from the 13th Abib to the 17th Abib, spanning five days. As described in Exodus 12 and Leviticus 23, the Passover and Feast of Unleavened Bread followed a specific timeline. The events unfolded from the 13th to the 21st of Abib, with significant days including the 14th (Passover), 15th (First Day of Unleavened Bread), and 21st (High Day Sabbath).

We'll discuss the implications of the seventh day of the week being the weekly Sabbath later. For now, let's acknowledge the seventh day of the week as the weekly Sabbath. Assuming the High Day Sabbath fell on Thursday, this creates an interesting scenario: only one day, Friday, separates the two Sabbaths – the first day of the Feast of Unleavened Bread (Thursday) and the weekly Sabbath (Saturday). This implies two Sabbaths occurred within the same week, specifically on the 15th and 17th of Abib.

Furthermore, given that the High Day Sabbaths occupied the first and seventh positions of the Feast of Unleavened Bread, we notice a remarkable concentration of Sabbaths: three within a seven-day period - specifically, Thursday (High Day Sabbath), Saturday (weekly Sabbath), and another High Day Sabbath on the seventh day of the feast (21st Abib).

For future reference, let's note the sequence of days:

The day of preparation fell on Tuesday, the 13th of Abib.

The Passover day was on Wednesday, the 14th of Abib.

The first day of the Feast of Unleavened Bread began on Thursday, the 15th of Abib, which was a High Day Sabbath.

Friday, the 16th of Abib, was the day after the High Day Sabbath and preceded the weekly Sabbath.

Finally, Saturday, the 17th of Abib, marked the weekly Sabbath.

We'll keep this sequence in mind for later discussions.

As we've observed, the initial mention of the Sabbath was in the context of the Feast of Unleavened Bread, specifically its first, which followed the Passover. Notably, the Passover itself prefigured the crucifixion of Jesus Christ, who would later be crucified on the same date, 14 Abib. This Passover week sequence of events underscores Jesus Christ's role as the ultimate fulfillment of God's redemptive plan.

As Scripture reveals, Jesus Christ became our Passover lamb (1 Corinthians 5:7-8), fulfilling the symbolism of the original Passover (Exodus 12). The Feast of Unleavened Bread's Sabbath days bookend this pivotal event, highlighting Jesus' role as the culmination of God's redemptive plan.

Why wasn't the Sabbath mentioned before the Passover and the Feast of Unleavened Bread?

After six days of creation, God rested on the seventh day, blessing and sanctifying it to commemorate His cessation from creative work. Notably, God did not initially command Adam and Eve to observe the seventh day. Instead, He reserved this instruction for the Exodus, when He chose a people to partner with in saving humanity.

At that point, the seventh day, though holy, was not yet designated for human observance. The focus was not on the day itself, but on its Lord – the One who voluntarily refrained from work, not out of fatigue, for God does not tire. His rest foreshadowed the ultimate rest awaiting humanity upon completing their earthly assignments.

Why did Jesus Christ call himself 'the Lord of the Sabbath'?

Jesus, as Lord of the Sabbath (Matthew 12:8), clarifies its purpose, stating, "The Sabbath was made for man, not man for the Sabbath" (Mark 2:27). This assertion emphasizes the Sabbath's human-centered focus, underscoring its institution for humanity's benefit, rather than for God's.

Exploring Jesus Christ's role as Lord of the Sabbath begins with understanding the purpose of the Sabbath. Why was it to be observed? Was it in honor of someone, and if so, who? Considering the Passover's symbolism, pointing to Jesus Christ's ultimate crucifixion as the Lamb of God, provides insight.

The first day following the initial Passover night was the initial Sabbath, honoring the Passover lamb, who foreshadowed Jesus Christ, the ultimate sacrificial lamb.

Jesus Christ is the Lord honored throughout the ages, from the Exodus for the Jews and from creation for humanity. As stated in Scripture, all was created by Him, for Him, and through Him; nothing was created without Him. He rested on the seventh day, establishing Himself as the Lord of the Sabbath.

This lordship began with the Sabbath's establishment following Passover, continued with its clarification after six days of manna, and was reaffirmed through its commission as one of Israel's Ten Commandments, given by the Lord who liberated them from Egyptian slavery.

Yes, as the Creator, Jesus Christ's authority over the Sabbath is rooted in His role in creation (John 1:3, Colossians 1:16-17). The Sabbath's institution honors Him, from the initial Passover to its reaffirmation in the Ten Commandments. Through His sacrifice, Jesus Christ became the ultimate fulfillment of the Passover lamb and Lord of the Sabbath.

Why did Jesus Christ say the Sabbath was made for man, not man for Sabbath?

Jesus' statement, "The Sabbath was made for man, not man for the Sabbath," clarifies the distinction between Genesis 2:2-3 and Exodus 20:8-11. In Genesis, God rested, whereas in Exodus, man is commanded to rest in honor of God's cessation from creation.

This distinction is crucial: God's rest on the seventh day was a one-time event, foreshadowing humanity's ultimate rest at the end of time. It wasn't the inception of an ongoing Sabbath observance for God, who continues to work.

Exodus 31:17 presents a profound statement: "It is a sign between me and the children of Israel forever: for in six days the LORD made heaven and earth, and on the seventh day He rested, and was refreshed."

Does this verse imply God rested due to weariness or did He mark the completion of initial creation? The phrase "was refreshed" sparks curiosity.

Was God refreshed because He was weary, or did He revitalize creation, enabling it to reproduce and renew itself on the eighth day? The latter interpretation aligns with God's omnipotence.

The Hebrew word for "refreshed" (yinnafash) means "to take breath" or "to revive." In this context, it suggests God revitalized creation, imbuing it with the power to replicate and flourish.

This understanding resonates with Genesis 2:2-3, where God blesses and sanctifies the seventh day, making it a day of rest and rejuvenation.

God's rest wasn't born of exhaustion but signaled the culmination of creation's foundation. On the eighth day, a new cycle began, mirroring the initial seven days, as creation started reproducing and evolving.

Thus, Exodus 31:17 highlights God's sovereign control, creative power, and loving provision for humanity.

The story of Noah's Flood (Genesis 6-9) illustrates that God's initial rest on the seventh day was a one-time event, not a recurring pattern. The rain poured down for 40 days and 40 nights (Genesis 7:12), and the floodwaters prevailed for 150 days (Genesis 7:24; 8:3). This prolonged event demonstrates that God's initial rest on the seventh day of the creation week was not a perpetual pattern. Even today, rains can fall on the Sabbath, illustrating that the Sabbath was instituted for humanity's benefit, not God's. The blessing of the seventh day held a deeper significance than merely the literal seventh day of every week. After all, God continues to work every day.

As Jesus stated in John 5:17, 'My Father is always working.' This truth is evident in the story of Noah's Flood, where the rain and floodwaters disregarded the weekly cycle.

In essence, Jesus' words emphasize that the Sabbath serves humanity's needs, not God's. God's rest was a deliberate cessation from creation, not an ongoing Sabbath observance. The Sabbath's purpose is to benefit humanity, providing rest and rejuvenation.

And so, Jesus' teaching in Mark 2:27 highlights the Sabbath's human-centered focus. While God rested after creation (Genesis 2:2-3), this wasn't the beginning of an ongoing Sabbath for Him. Instead, the Sabbath was instituted at the Exodus (Exodus 20:8-11) as a blessing for humanity, foreshadowing ultimate rest in Him (Hebrews 4:9-11).

Before proceeding, let's delve into the essence of God's rest on the seventh day. Was He truly idle, or was something more profound unfolding?

When we rest, do we spend the entire day in inactivity? Or do we find refreshment, peace, joy, and happiness in moments of stillness? Isn't rest a time for meditation, self-reflection, and introspection?

Consider this: When did God create intangible virtues like peace, joy, happiness, and love? Were they not birthed during the seventh day, as God rested from physical creation?

Perhaps the seventh day represents the replication and reproduction of spiritual virtues, mirroring the pattern of the previous six days. Just as the physical world continues to reproduce and renew itself, the seventh day may symbolize the ongoing creation and cultivation of spiritual life.

On the seventh day, God's rest was not a state of inactivity, but a transformative moment. He was busy cultivating peace, joy, and happiness, planting seeds that would bloom in the hearts of His creation.

As He rested, God established a sacred rhythm, teaching the world the value of stillness and rejuvenation. In this quiet moment, He modeled the importance of self-reflection and introspection, inviting humanity to pause and examine their souls.

With gentle care, God infused creation with spiritual vitality, breathing life into the essence of all that existed. And as He did, He reproduced and renewed spiritual virtues, nurturing love, compassion, and kindness to flourish in the world.

In this restful moment, God's creative power took on a new form, shaping the inner landscape of humanity. His seventh-day rest became a gift, offering a blueprint for balance, harmony, and spiritual growth – a testament to the beauty of stillness and the transformative power of divine love.

In this light, God's rest becomes an invitation to embrace the beauty of stillness, reflection, and spiritual growth.

Here, note that the first and seventh days of creation hold distinct significance. On the first day, God created light, an invisible entity that causes visibility, illuminating the world and making other creations visible. This divine light is inaccessible, infinite, and spiritual, paving the way for the subsequent creations over the next five days.

In stark contrast, the seventh day was marked by God's rest. Yet, during this apparent stillness, He created something equally profound: the invisible, yet essential, necessities that sustain humanity. On this day, God established the fulfillment of humanity's deepest needs and desires, crafting elements that make life worthwhile and indispensable to human experience.

While the first day's light illuminated the physical world, the seventh day's creations nurtured humanity's spiritual, emotional, and relational well-being. These intangible gifts include peace, rest, relaxation, joy, love, and purpose – the very things that make life meaningful and fulfilling.

Together, the first and seventh days bookend God's creative work, highlighting the interconnectedness of physical and spiritual sustenance. As the divine light illuminates our surroundings, God's seventh-day creations illuminate our souls.

Leviticus 23:7-8 notably echoes the uniqueness of the first and seventh days of creation. The passage describes two special Sabbaths following the Passover, a pivotal event that foreshadowed the Crucifixion of Jesus Christ, the Redeemer and ultimate Sabbath.

Just as the first day brought forth light and the seventh day brought rest, the Passover Sabbaths symbolize redemption and spiritual rest. The first Sabbath commemorates the Israelites' deliverance from Egypt, while the seventh-day Sabbath represents the culmination of God's plan of salvation.

In Jesus Christ, these themes converge: He is the light of the world, the source of redemption, and the ultimate Sabbath rest for humanity.

CHAPTER four

Manna Sabbath vs Weekly Sabbath

The Sabbath's origins are rooted in Israel's history, with initial instructions given during Passover (Exodus 12, 15th Abib), followed by its introduction during manna distribution (Exodus 16, 22nd Iyar), and its institutionalization as a weekly observance (Exodus 20 and Deuteronomy 5).

The Bible presents a multifaceted understanding of the Sabbath, with Exodus 20 and Deuteronomy 5 providing two distinct reasons for its observation. God's rest on the seventh day (Exodus 20:11) and Israel's deliverance from Egyptian slavery (Deuteronomy 5:15) serve as foundational rationales.

The manna Sabbath (Exodus 16:23-30) follows, where God provided manna in the wilderness, and the Sabbath was observed as a day of rest, foreshadowing God's provision and care. Finally, the weekly Sabbath command (Exodus 20:8-11, Deuteronomy 5:12-15) was given as part of the Ten Commandments, linking it to God's creation rest (Genesis 2:2-3) and the Israelites' redemption from slavery.

We will now examine the two seventh-day Sabbaths mentioned in Exodus - the Manna Sabbath in Exodus 16 and the weekly Sabbath in Exodus 20 - to determine whether they refer to the same day or distinct observances.

This examination will help clarify the connection between the Manna Sabbath, where Israel learned to rest and trust God's provision (Exodus 16), and the weekly Sabbath, instituted as a perpetual covenant (Exodus 20). Understanding their relationship sheds light on the biblical Sabbath's significance and observance.

Let's take a step back and focus on the period preceding Moses's time and the Exodus. There is no explicit evidence in the biblical text that the Sabbath was observed prior to the Exodus. In fact, the Sabbath is not mentioned at all in the book of Genesis, except for God's rest on the seventh day in Genesis 2:2-3. Although the uniqueness of the seventh day has its roots in creation, when God rested on it, blessed it as holy, and resumed his work on the eighth day, starting a new cycle of weeks, in the early dispensations, there is no explicit command to observe it.

Interestingly, the Bible remains silent on the days of the week from the creation account in Genesis 1-2 until the institution of the seventh-day Sabbath in Exodus 16. This significant gap spans over 2000 years, encompassing the patriarchal era, including the stories of Abraham, Isaac, Jacob, and Joseph.

This omission suggests that, prior to Exodus 16, the Israelites did not observe or emphasize the days of the week. Instead, their calendar focused on lunar cycles, with importance placed on months, their year beginning in the first month, later named Tishrei, before Abib/Nisan was rescheduled the first month of their sacred year.

The lack of reference to weekdays implies that the ancient Hebrews organized their time around lunar phases and annual festivals, rather than a weekly cycle.

Exodus 16 marks a turning point, where God reintroduces the seventh-day, calling it a Sabbath, emphasizing its significance (Exodus 16:26-30).

The absence of weekday mentions between Genesis 2 and Exodus 16 raises questions about pre-Exodus Sabbath observance. The creation account introduces the seven-day week, but biblical records do not explicitly indicate that the Israelites followed the modern weekday sequence (Sunday to Saturday) prior to the Exodus. The lack of reference to weekdays before the Exodus implies that the Israelites might not have placed significance on the weekly cycle or observed the sequence of the days of the week.

Two distinct reasons for Sabbath observance are provided in Scripture, the creation rest (Exodus 20:8-11): God rested on the seventh day and sanctified it. However, this passage does not imply that humanity was commanded to observe the Sabbath at that time.

The second reason for Sabbath observance is the deliverance from Egypt (Deuteronomy 5:12-15): God's liberation of Israel from bondage served as the second justification.

The biblical narrative suggests that Sabbath observance began almost at the beginning of the Exodus, specifically from Iyar 22nd in the Exodus year. This date coincides with the manna's cessation on the seventh day (Exodus 16:26-30).

Given these considerations, it is reasonable to conclude that the seventh-day Sabbath, as a commanded observance, began with the Israelites just after the start of the Exodus, rather than being an ongoing practice since creation.

Furthermore, Exodus 12 doesn't specify the sequence of weekdays, but instead focuses on the seven-day observance of Unleavened Bread, with the first and seventh days designated as Sabbaths or holy convocations, based on the Abib calendar. In contrast, Exodus 16 introduces the modern weekly cycle, identifying the seventh day through the manna's cessation.

In a parallel to creation, God rested on the seventh day by withholding manna, establishing the Sabbath. This weekly rhythm continued for 40 years, with God refraining from providing manna and the Israelites refraining from collecting it.

Once the Israelites adjusted to this weekly pattern, God incorporated Sabbath observance into the Ten Commandments. Even after the manna ceased, the seventh-day Sabbath persisted, becoming an enduring part of Israel's tradition.

Let's reiterate for clarity. In the dispensation of Adam and Eve, God forbade them from eating the fruit of the tree of knowledge, but there is no mention of the Sabbath. Similarly, in the dispensation of Noah, God commands him to build the Ark, but the Sabbath is not mentioned. This raises interesting questions about the relationship between pre-Exodus patriarchal worship practices and the institutionalized Sabbath observance that began
with the Exodus.

However, Genesis 12:1-3 records the pivotal moment when God called Abram, launching a new dispensation that would shape the course of salvation history. Abram's response marked the beginning of a special covenant, establishing him as the father of God's chosen people.

God established a covenant with Abram, promising to make him the father of a great nation (Genesis 12:2-3). This covenant was reaffirmed with Abram's son Isaac (Genesis 26:2-5) and later with his grandchild Jacob (Genesis 28:13-15).

Notably, during this dispensation, known as the Patriarchal Dispensation, neither the Sabbath nor the week days are explicitly mentioned. God's focus was on establishing His relationship with Abram, Isaac, and Jacob, and shaping the nascent nation of Israel. The covenant promises centered on land, descendants, and blessings, without any reference to Sabbath observance or any other holy day.

In this dispensation, God also introduced circumcision as a sign of the covenant (Genesis 17:9-14), which would become an essential aspect of Jewish identity. The Patriarchs' stories, marked by faith, obedience, and promise, paved the way for the eventual giving of the Law, including the Sabbath commandment, to the Israelites in the wilderness.

This period of God's relationship with the Patriarchs demonstrates His patience, guidance, and preparation for the nation's future. The absence of Sabbath mention during this time underscores God's focus on building relationships, making covenants, and setting the stage for the fuller revelation of His laws and plans.

The New Testament often fills in gaps and provides additional insights not explicitly mentioned in the Old Testament, while also affirming and validating many of its teachings. For instance, in John 4:12 and 20, the Samaritan woman acknowledges the historical significance of Jacob's well and the ancestral worship practices in the mountains, demonstrating continuity between the Old and New Testaments.

However, regarding Sabbath observance, the biblical record suggests that there is no explicit evidence or clear pointer to its observance before the Exodus era.

The New Testament affirms the Sabbath's significance, which originated in the Exodus era, and highlights Jesus Christ's fulfillment and redefinition of the Sabbath (Matthew 12:8, Mark 2:27-28, Luke 13:10-17). As a result, the early Christian community transitioned to observing the Lord's Day (Sunday) as a day of worship and rest.

However, there are a few instances where the patriarchs' stories are referenced, although not necessarily in the context of Sabbath discussions. In Matthew 24:20, Jesus refers to the Sabbath when discussing future tribulation, but does not link it to the patriarchs. In Acts 7:2-53, Stephen's speech mentions the patriarchs exclusively, but omits any mention of Sabbath observance. Hebrews 4:9-10 mentions the Sabbath rest, but in the context of Jesus Christ being the true Sabbath rest, without specifically linking it to the patriarchs.

Similarly, in Galatians 3:6-29, Paul discusses the faith of the patriarchs without mentioning Sabbath observance. In Romans 4:9-22, Paul references Abraham's faith, but does not connect it to Sabbath keeping.

The New Testament primarily focuses on the life, teachings, death, and resurrection of Jesus Christ and the spread of Christianity. Although it acknowledges the patriarchs as important figures in God's plan, it does not explicitly link them to Sabbath observance.

It isn't until Exodus 16:23, after the Israelites gathered manna for six days, that the provision rested on the seventh day, the Sabbath of the Lord. This marks the first explicit mention of the Sabbath rest for humanity. The pattern of work and rest established in creation is now applied to humanity, foreshadowing the ultimate rest that comes through Jesus Christ.

Throughout the dispensations, God's focus has been on establishing his relationship with humanity, making covenants, and guiding his chosen people. The Sabbath, however, remains a consistent theme, pointing to the ultimate rest that comes through Jesus Christ. The transition from one dispensation to another highlights God's progressive revelation, ultimately leading to the fulfillment of rest in Jesus Christ.

According to Exodus 16:1-36, the Israelites departed from Elim and arrived in the Wilderness of Sin on the fifteenth day of the second month, Iyar (Exodus 16:1). This was approximately one month after leaving Egypt, where they had observed the Passover and the Feast of Unleavened Bread, which began on the fifteenth day of the first month, Abib (Exodus 12:15-20, Leviticus 23:5-7).

Assuming the Israelites left Egypt on the fifteenth day of Abib, this encounter in the Wilderness of Sin occurred around the sixteenth day of Iyar. The timing suggests that the Sabbath of the Feast of Unleavened Bread (fifteenth day of Abib) and the manna Sabbath (twenty-second day of Iyar) were likely separated by about five weeks.

This distinction highlights the development of Israel's understanding of the Sabbath. Initially tied to the Feast of Unleavened Bread and their liberation from Egypt, the Sabbath now becomes linked to God's daily provision and care in the wilderness.

The Manna Sabbath count commenced on 16 Iyar in the year of the Exodus, with the first Manna Sabbath occurring on 22 Iyar, exactly seven days later. This alignment recurs every 19 years. An important inquiry remains: Was the initial Manna Sabbath synchronized with the creation weekly seventh day? This question will be explored subsequently.

To help us reach an answer, and given the manna Sabbath's absence in subsequent events, we must acknowledge that the manna Sabbath also prefigures God's later instruction to observe the weekly Sabbath, as expressed in the Ten Commandments (Exodus 20:8-11, Deuteronomy 5:12-15). This instruction emphasizes both God's rest during creation and Israel's redemption from slavery, underscoring the Sabbath's profound significance in Israel's worship and identity.

The formal command to observe the Sabbath, as we discussed earlier, is given in Exodus 20:8-11, as part of the Ten Commandments. It's worth noting that the Sabbath becomes a distinctive feature of Israelite worship and identity after the Exodus, serving as a reminder of their covenant with God and their deliverance from slavery in Egypt.

When God gave the Ten Commandments, He explicitly introduced Himself, establishing His identity and authority. He addressed a specific people, the Israelites, with whom He had a prior relationship, reminding them of His mighty acts and deliverance.

As recorded in Exodus 20:1-3, God began by declaring, "I am the Lord your God, who brought you out of the land of Egypt, out of the house of bondage." By introducing Himself as their Deliverer, God reminded the Israelites of His miraculous intervention in their lives, specifically referencing their liberation from Egyptian slavery. This reminder served as a foundation for the commandments that followed.

The first commandment, "You shall have no other gods before Me," emphasized the Israelites' exclusive allegiance to Yahweh, the Lord. This command established monotheism and rejected polytheism, which was prevalent in ancient Egyptian and Mesopotamian cultures.

By starting with this command, God asserted His sovereignty and uniqueness, established a covenant relationship with Israel, rejected idolatry and false worship, and set the tone for the remaining commandments, emphasizing loyalty, obedience, and moral responsibility. This initial commandment also underscored the significance of worshiping the one true

God, who created the universe, delivered Israel from slavery, and entered into a covenant with Abraham, Isaac, and Jacob.

By remembering God's mighty acts and heeding the first commandment, the Israelites demonstrated their gratitude, loyalty, and commitment to their covenant Lord. This introduction and first commandment laid the groundwork for the Israelites' relationship with God, defining their obligations and responsibilities as His chosen people.

Now, let's consider two separate seventh-day rests described in Scripture: the "manna Sabbath" in Exodus 16, where manna skipped the day, and the "weekly Sabbath" commanded in the Ten Commandments (Exodus 20:8-11 and Deuteronomy 5:12-15). Analyzing the distinctions between these two Sabbaths yields important insights.

The events surrounding the seventh day in the book of Genesis are distinct and serve different purposes. Firstly, God rested on the seventh day, ceasing from His creative work (Genesis 2:2-3). This act of rest was a divine initiative, separate from human involvement.

Next, God blessed the seventh day and sanctified it (Genesis 2:3), setting it apart as a special day. This blessing and sanctification were also divine actions, independent of human participation.

Lastly, the commandment to observe the seventh day as a day of rest and keep it holy was given to God's people, the Israelites, after they had been established as a nation (Exodus 20:8-11, Deuteronomy 5:12-15). This commandment was a part of the covenant between God and His people, and its purpose was to commemorate God's creation and redemption.

And so, the resting, blessing, and sanctifying of the seventh day were divine actions, while the commandment to observe and keep it holy was a directive given to God's people. These are distinct aspects, each serving a unique purpose in the broader narrative of God's relationship with humanity.

The question persists: was the Sabbath observed prior to the Exodus? The simple answer is 'No'. Before the Exodus, there are instances where work continued for extended periods without rest. A notable example is Abram's pursuit of Chedorlaomer and his allies after Lot's abduction (Genesis 14:13-16). This campaign likely lasted more than a week.

Consider the distances involved: Abram operated from the plain of Mamre, near Hebron (Genesis 13:18, 14:13). The journey from Hebron to

Hobah, near Damascus, spans approximately 210 miles (338 km). Assuming a moderate pace of 20-25 miles (32-40 km) per day, Abram's round trip, including battle time, could have taken two weeks or more.

This scenario suggests that Sabbath rest may not have been observed during this time. Rather, the Sabbath was instituted during the Exodus as a gift for humanity.

Why was the Sabbath instituted as late as the Exodus era?

The Sabbath's introduction during the Exodus era served a specific purpose: to commemorate God's creation and redemption. This commandment honored Jesus Christ, the Creator (John 1:3) and Redeemer (1 Corinthians 5:7-8), who would ultimately fulfill the Sabbath's promise of rest.

Let's explore the true meaning and significance of the Sabbath, regardless of whether it falls on the seventh day or another day. What is the purpose and importance of observing the Sabbath?

The biblical timeline reveals a fascinating sequence of events. Since Jesus Christ, the Messiah, was destined to be the firstborn of all creation (Colossians 1:15) and the fulfillment of God's plans, the Sabbath of the Feast of Unleavened Bread holds a significant position in the chronology of God's redemptive plan. Before the manna Sabbath and the weekly Sabbath command, which may be one and the same, the Sabbath of the Feast of Unleavened Bread comes first. This Sabbath commemorates the Israelites' liberation from Egyptian bondage and foreshadows Christ's ultimate redemption.

The sequence of events underscores Jesus Christ's role as the ultimate fulfillment of God's plans. The Sabbath of the Feast of Unleavened Bread (Exodus 12:15-20, Leviticus 23:5-7) marks the beginning of the Israelites' journey out of Egypt, symbolizing redemption and freedom. The manna Sabbath (Exodus 16:23-30) follows, where God provided manna in the wilderness, and the Sabbath was observed as a day of rest, foreshadowing God's provision and care. Finally, the weekly Sabbath command (Exodus 20:8-11, Deuteronomy 5:12-15) was given as part of the Ten Commandments, linking it to God's creation rest (Genesis 2:2-3) and the Israelites' redemption from slavery.

As the firstborn of all creation, Jesus Christ is the embodiment of redemption, provision, and rest. The Sabbath of the Feast of Unleavened Bread, the manna Sabbath, and the weekly Sabbath all point to His redemptive work.

In Jesus Christ, the Sabbath finds its ultimate meaning and fulfillment, as He declares, "The Son of Man is Lord of the Sabbath" (Matthew 12:8).

And so, Exodus 16:23-30 contains the first explicit reference to the seventh day Sabbath, with Moses instructing the Israelites to rest on the seventh day after collecting manna for six days. Notably, this passage presents a transitional phase, introducing the Sabbath concept without formally mandating its observance.

The formal command to observe the Sabbath was given in Exodus 20:8-11 and Deuteronomy 5:12-15, as part of the Ten Commandments. This command linked the Sabbath to God's creation rest and the Israelites' redemption from slavery. The day's significance lies not in its inherent holiness but in its designation as a time to honor the Holy One.

The Sabbath finds its ultimate meaning and fulfillment in Jesus Christ, who declared, "The Son of Man is Lord of the Sabbath" (Matthew 12:8). The Sabbath of the Feast of Unleavened Bread, the manna Sabbath, and the weekly Sabbath all point to His redemptive work.

The question remains, is the manna Sabbath the same with the weekly Sabbath since they were both observed on the seventh day?

To determine if the Manna Sabbath coincided with the weekly Sabbath, we must examine the initial dates of the Exodus, traditionally dated to 1446 BCE, and verify if the weekdays align. According to Exodus 16:4 and 14-15, God began providing manna on the sixteenth day of the second month, Iyar. Moses then instructed the Israelites to collect manna for six days, reserving the seventh day for rest and sanctification (Exodus 16:23-26). The crucial question is: did the Manna Sabbath fall on the seventh day of the week, which would be Saturday, the traditional weekly Sabbath?

Using the Hebrew calendar, which traditionally dates the Exodus to 1446 BCE, we can calculate the weekdays corresponding to the Manna Sabbath. If the sixteenth day of Iyar fell on a Sunday, the Manna Sabbath would have been on Saturday, aligning with the traditional weekly Sabbath.

Before proceeding, let's examine the connection between God's rest during the creation week and the Manna Sabbath rest in Exodus 16.

In the creation week, God rested on the seventh day, not in idleness, but in sovereign provision. Similarly, during the Manna Sabbath, God "rested" by withholding manna, signifying His cessation from daily provision (Exodus 16).

Although some Israelites disregarded God's implied rest and searched for manna, they found none (Exodus 16:27). God addressed their disobedience, clarifying His intention to teach Sabbath observance through the manna's provision (Exodus 16:28-30).

Interestingly, those who disobeyed the Manna Sabbath rest were not severed from Israel, contrasting with the severe consequences for disregarding the Passover/Unleavened Bread commandment.

The Passover, foreshadowing Jesus Christ's crucifixion, burial, and resurrection, demanded strict adherence. Disobedience resulted in being "cut off from Israel" (Exodus 12:15, 19), emphasizing the gravity of neglecting this pivotal feast.

In contrast, the Manna Sabbath's gentle introduction allowed for instruction and correction, rather than immediate punishment. This distinction highlights God's pedagogical approach, teaching the Israelites through provision and guidance before formalizing the Sabbath commandment (Exodus 20:8-11).

This contrast also underscores the unique significance of the Passover, as a foreshadowing of Jesus Christ's redemptive work, and the importance of faithful participation in this foundational feast.

Despite the people's disobedience, God mercifully overlooked their transgression and graciously met their needs. He supplied double the manna on the sixth day, preparing the Israelites for the weekly Sabbath rest.

This rehearsal prepared the Israelites for the Sabbath command, a lasting covenant.

The Manna week paralleled the creation week, where God rested on the seventh day. This parallel reveals God's consistent character: resting yet providing, ceasing work yet sustaining His people.

CHAPTER five

The Year of the Exodus

In the biblical timeline, the assumed year of the beginning of the Exodus, 1446 BCE (2315 AM), marked two significant events: the Exodus from Egypt and, notably, the initiation of manna in the wilderness.

During the Exodus, the Israelites observed the Passover and the Feast of Unleavened Bread, beginning on 15 Abib (Thursday), with the weekly Sabbath falling on Saturday, the 17th of Abib.

Later, in the Wilderness of Sin, God provided manna starting on 16 Iyar (Thursday), approximately one month after leaving Egypt. This provision continued for six days, ceasing on Tuesday, and making Wednesday, the 22nd of Iyar, a day of rest – the Sabbath to the Lord (Exodus 16:1-30).

Notably, this Wednesday Sabbath preceded the formal institution of the weekly Sabbath as part of the Ten Commandments (Exodus 20:8-11, Deuteronomy 5:12-15). Until the manna ceased, the Israelites observed this 22 Iyar Sabbath.

A question arises: did they, in 1446 BCE, observe both Wednesday and Saturday as rest days, or did they adopt a new weekly cycle beginning with 16 Iyar as the first day (equivalent to Sunday in today's reckoning), making the 22nd of Iyar the seventh day (equivalent to Saturday today)? This would imply the Israelites counted their weeks from the initiation of manna.

The biblical text does not provide explicit clarification, but further examination of the biblical calendar and Sabbath observance may shed light on this inquiry.

In ancient Hebrew culture, days were numbered rather than named, facilitating varied interpretations of biblical texts. This numerical system also allowed for periodic resets, as seen in 1446 BCE when the Israelites were instructed to start their sacred year from Abib, despite being mid-year. Similarly, the manna's onset may have reset the seven-day cycle, potentially beginning on Wednesday, aligning with the creation week's fourth day. This would distinguish the natural calendar's seventh day from the manna seventh day, reflecting the intricate interplay between sacred and calendar cycles in ancient Hebrew timekeeping.

The relationship between the Wednesday Sabbath and the later institutionalized weekly Sabbath remains an intriguing topic for further exploration, particularly in understanding the development of Israel's worship practices and calendar observances.

Assuming the Manna Sabbath coincided with the weekly Sabbath, it would reveal a conflict between the sacred Jewish calendar's weekly cycle and the Jewish Civil calendar's weekly cycle. This discrepancy would cause weekdays, including the seventh day, to fall on different days. The biblical account, however, indicates that the Sabbath was specifically ordained for the Jewish people, meaning its observance would follow the sacred calendar, rather than the civil or any other calendar.

This raises doubts about the traditional view that the weekly cycle has remained continuous since creation, unaffected by alterations to calendars.

As we have seen, attempts to reconcile the Manna Sabbath and weekly Sabbath using the 1446 BCE calendar setup encounter significant challenges. The Sabbaths fail to align, prompting questions about their relationship.

For approximately 40 years, the Israelites observed the Manna Sabbath without distinction from the weekly Sabbath. This implies that the Manna Sabbath was, in fact, the same Sabbath observed weekly. If two separate Sabbaths existed per week, the Israelites would have gathered manna for only five days to avoid working on both the Manna Sabbath and the weekly Sabbath. Instead, the biblical account indicates they gathered manna for six days, suggesting a single Sabbath observance per week, supplemented by occasional high holy day Sabbaths.

The Israelites' 40-year observance of the Manna Sabbath supports its identity as the weekly Sabbath rather than an additional, distinct Sabbath. This understanding underscores the unity of Sabbath observance in the Israelites' experience.

Therefore, as previously suggested, 1446 BCE (2315 AM) may not be the initial year of the Exodus. This is a potential indication that the traditional timeline requires revision.

To overcome the synchronization challenge, let's adopt a two-step approach. Due to the Hebrew calendar's 19-year cycle, we can simplify our search. Let's first identify a recent year where the Manna Sabbath and weekly

Sabbath synchronize, then apply this pattern to years surrounding 1446 BCE to potentially pinpoint the Exodus year.

The year 2023 AD/CE serves as an illustrative example, assuming the creation week's sequence remained intact without restarting on any day other than Sunday, the first day of the week. In 2023, the Passover fell on Wednesday, 14th Abib/Nissan (5 April), marking the beginning of the Feast of Unleavened Bread on Thursday, 15th Abib, a high holy day Sabbath.

The subsequent days unfolded as follows: Friday was a non-Sabbath day, and Saturday, 17th Abib, was a weekly Sabbath (8 April 2023). According to Exodus 16, the manna provision commenced on 16th Iyar. In 2023, this date corresponded to Sunday, 7 May.

Significantly, counting from 16th Iyar, the seventh-day manna Sabbath fell on 22nd Iyar, Saturday, 13 May 2023. This alignment with the regular weekly Sabbath supports the notion that the Exodus initial year had a similar calendar setup to 2023 AD/CE.

Considering the traditional Exodus date of 1446 BCE, a focused examination of years closest to this timeframe reveals potential candidates for the initial Exodus year. Specifically, aligning 22 Iyar with Saturday narrows down the options. Among these, one year stands out:1456 BCE (2305 AM), and

1435 BCE (2326 AM), positioned 10 years before and 11 years after the traditionally accepted 1446 BCE, respectively.

Notably, our analysis reveals that 1435 BCE presents a compelling case for the Exodus year due to its unique calendar alignment, and supporting perspectives from notable researchers such as Dr. Gerald A. Aardsma, whose biblical and astronomical analyses align with our findings.

On this year, 16 Iyar fell on a Sunday, making 22 Iyar, the seventh-day rest from manna gathering, coincide with Saturday, the seventh day of the week, specifically May 30, 1435 BCE. This synchronization suggests that 1435 BCE could potentially be the initial year of the Exodus.

Historical context supports this alignment. The Pharaohs of the 18th dynasty, notably Thutmose III (1479-1425 BCE), provide a backdrop for the Exodus narrative. Archaeological findings, such as the Ipuwer Papyrus and the Merneptah Stele, offer additional evidence.

Calendrical details are crucial. The Hebrew calendar's 19-year Metonic cycle ensures that the Sabbath falls on the same day of the week every 19 years. This cycle, combined with the 7-day week, guides researchers in identifying potential Exodus years.

If this is the case, then both the current Jewish Sacred and Civil calendars would be accurate, resolving the apparent discrepancy.

The Manna Sabbath and weekly Sabbath may be one and the same. Its initiation on 22nd Iyar 1435 BCE notwithstanding, the Manna Sabbath was not date- or lunar-dependent. Rather, it followed a counting pattern akin to the weekly Sabbath, anchored to a specific starting point. Thus, the Sabbath continues uninterrupted, whereas the manna supply ceased. This aligns with Exodus 20, where the Sabbath commandment is given. This understanding resolves the apparent distinction between the Manna Sabbath and weekly Sabbath.

Jesus' profound teaching in Mark 2:27 underscores the Sabbath's fundamental human-centered purpose, applicable to all Sabbaths, including the high day Sabbath, the Manna Sabbath, and the weekly Sabbath. The first Sabbath mentioned in Scripture, the initial day of the Feast of Unleavened Bread (Exodus 12:15-16, Leviticus 23:5-7), and the final day of the same feast (Exodus 12:15-20, Leviticus 23:8), uniquely honored the Lamb slain from the foundation of the world – Jesus Christ (Revelation 13:8, 1 Peter 1:19-20). Similarly, the Manna Sabbath commemorated the divine provision of Israel's needs, recognizing God as the Provider who miraculously supplied manna, often described as 'angel's food' (Psalm 78:25).

The Sabbath commandment in Exodus 20:8-11 was instituted not only as a reminder of God's creation rest (Exodus 20:11) but also as a blessing for humanity, foreshadowing the ultimate rest found in Jesus Christ (Hebrews 4:9-11). This Sabbath rest symbolized deliverance from the burdens of sin and the world, pointing to the eternal rest secured through Jesus' redemptive work.

In this context, Jesus' statement in Mark 2:27, 'The Sabbath was made for man, not man for the Sabbath,' reaffirms the Sabbath's purpose as a gift to humanity, designed for our rejuvenation, spiritual renewal, and communion with our Creator.

A further consideration raises an important question: Does the 1435 BCE Exodus date, which aligns with global calendars, potentially conflict with God's purpose to distinguish Israel from other nations? Leviticus 20:26 and Deuteronomy 7:6 emphasize God's desire to set Israel apart; but this alignment seems to contradict God's desire? It's possible he recalibrated the weekly schedule to start from the manna's inaugural day, effectively making it the new first day of the week. If so, why wouldn't He adjust the weekday sequence to align with the Israelites' unique calendar, which begins mid-year? In this sense, despite discrepancies in Sabbath alignment with the Jewish civil calendar, 1446 BCE remains a viable candidate for the actual year of the Exodus.

Consider the fact that God rescheduled the Israelites' year to commence in spring, diverging from prevailing ancient Near Eastern calendars, as stated in Exodus 12:2 and 23:16.

The Manna Sabbath's introduction in Exodus 16:1-36 implies a new weekly rhythm. Why provide fresh instructions if this day already coincided with an existing day of rest? Additionally, the absence of subsequent Manna Sabbath mentions suggests it became the sole weekly Sabbath for the Israelites.

Two possible explanations emerge. The Jewish people, in later years, may have opted to maintain the traditional weekday sequence, aligning with surrounding nations, while observing holy days according to the lunar calendar. Alternatively, God may have intentionally separated the Israelites' weekly Sabbath from the traditional seventh day, establishing a unique rhythm for His chosen people.

Scriptural context supports this distinction, emphasizing Israel's unique status among nations in Exodus 19:5-6, Leviticus 20:22-26, and Deuteronomy 7:6-11.

In Exodus 19:5-6 and 1 Peter 2:9, God unequivocally states that being a peculiar people, a chosen generation, a holy nation, and a royal priesthood requires obeying His voice and keeping His covenant. To be set apart, one must diverge from the majority's practices. Israel had to adhere to God's commandments, including the Ten Commandments and subsequent divine instructions.

A poignant illustration of this principle is found in Moses' experiences in the wilderness. In Exodus 17:5-7, God instructed Moses to strike the Rock with his rod to provide water for the Israelites in the wilderness of Sin. Later, in Numbers 20:7-12, God directed Moses to speak to the Rock, rather than strike it, to produce water in the wilderness of Zin. However, Moses repeated his previous action, striking the Rock instead of speaking to it. Despite the Rock still yielding water, God was displeased with Moses' disobedience, and this incident prevented him from entering Canaan (Numbers 20:12, 27:14).

This account underscores that with God, obedience supersedes consistency and practicality. The Rock, representing God's Faithfulness (Jesus Christ), provided water despite Moses' mistake, but Moses' disobedience resulted in dishonor.

The intersection of biblical narrative, historical context, and calendrical complexities invites ongoing exploration and discussion, raising questions about the nature of Sabbath observance in modern times and its connection to Israel's covenantal identity. This inquiry touches on fundamental aspects of biblical faith, including God's sovereignty over time, His distinction of Israel, and the enduring significance of the Sabbath.

As we delve deeper into this topic, we find ourselves navigating the intricate relationships between biblical history, cultural context, and divine guidance, ultimately seeking a deeper understanding of God's plan and its relevance to our lives today.

An ongoing concern, the traditional Exodus year of 1446 BCE, has long been a subject of debate among scholars and historians, with some arguing for alternative dates based on archaeological findings and biblical analysis. A crucial question emerges: is this date inaccurate, or did the world simply fail to align the weekday sequence with the new count initiated by the Manna Sabbath, as ordained by God? This oversight is not unprecedented.

Historical precedents demonstrate how calendar discrepancies can arise. For instance, the Venerable Bede and other scholars recognized flaws in Dionysius Exiguus' Anno Domini dating system. Instead of correcting the error, they placed Jesus Christ's birth year at 6 BCE, effectively setting the calendar six years askew. This anomaly has persisted, shaping our understanding of history.

Similarly, the Manna Sabbath's alignment may have been disregarded by later calendar developers. In their pursuit of consistency and practicality, they may have inadvertently disrupted the original sequence. The ancient Israelites, who meticulously observed the Manna Sabbath, would not have been responsible for this discrepancy.

The Hebrew calendar's complexities and variations over time contribute to the challenge. Lunar cycles, leap years, and intercalations have all impacted the calendar's accuracy. Scholars propose various solutions, including recalculating the Exodus year or re-examining the Sabbath's original alignment.

For instance, when God initiated the Israelites' new year in Egypt, beginning the Exodus (Exodus 12:2), He deliberately disrupted the traditional calendar flow. This six-month discrepancy has never been fully accounted for, yet the Hebrew calendar remains aligned with other calendars. This suggests that later generations of Israelites disregarded their unique calendar, which had a plus or minus six months due to the disruption.

The notion of overlooking errors for the sake of consistency and practicality is problematic, as evidenced by the unaccounted-for six-month discrepancy in this calendar.

This oversight raises significant concerns:

By prioritizing consistency and practicality over accuracy, the Israelites may have compromised the integrity of their calendar. This calendars discrepancy could have far-reaching implications for understanding biblical chronology, Sabbath observance, and covenant obligations.

The Hebrew calendar's continued alignment with other calendars implies a potential synchronization with external systems, rather than adherence to the original divine initiative. This synchronization may have resulted from a desire for convenience, cultural exchange, or political expediency.

However, this approach neglects the distinctive nature of the Israelites' covenant relationship with God. By dismissing the six-month discrepancy, the Israelites risked obscuring the historical and theological significance of God's actions in Egypt.

Furthermore, overlooking errors for practicality's sake can:

Create a slippery slope, where subsequent errors or adjustments are tolerated for the sake of convenience.

Undermine the authority of Scripture, which emphasizes the importance of precise timekeeping and covenant observance.

Obscure the nuances of biblical history, leading to inaccurate interpretations and misunderstandings.

And so, the unaccounted-for six-month discrepancy serves as a cautionary tale about the dangers of prioritizing consistency and practicality over accuracy.

By examining this discrepancy, we are reminded of the importance of fidelity to the original divine initiative and the need for precise understanding of biblical chronology and covenant obligations.

This historical context highlights the tension between adhering to divine instructions and conforming to established systems. While our calendars may appear efficient, we may be inadvertently disregarding God's original design.

The implications of this principle extend beyond calendar systems to our daily lives:

- Are we prioritizing obedience to God's voice or conforming to societal norms?

- Do we trust God's unconventional methods or rely on human wisdom?

The Israelites' decision to align their God-given calendar year with other nations' calendars, while maintaining the Hebrew Civil calendar, reflects a recurring pattern of conforming to worldly standards. This phenomenon is rooted in their history, marked by instances of rejecting God's sovereignty.

In 1 Samuel 8:4-22, the Israelites requested a human king, renouncing God as their earthly ruler, seeking to emulate other nations. God acquiesced, granting them Saul, who was later rejected in favor of David (1 Samuel 16:1-13). This desire for worldly alignment preceded a more profound rejection – that of the Messiah, Jesus Christ.

When Jesus arrived, the Israelites rejected Him, having preconceived notions of their expected Messiah (Luke 19:41-44, John 1:11). This rejection was tantamount to rejecting God Himself, echoing a familiar pattern. Jesus highlighted the Queen of the South's faithfulness, contrasting it with Israel's disobedience (Matthew 12:42, Luke 11:31).

The consequences of this rejection were far-reaching. The Gentiles were grafted onto the Jewish roots, replacing those who had been cut off for rejecting God (Romans 11:11-24). This shift underscores the universal nature of God's plan, extending beyond Israel's borders.

The biblical narrative reinforces a significant theme: Israel's complex relationship with God's sovereignty. This dynamic is illustrated through various passages, including Ezekiel 20:32-44, which highlights Israel's recurring rejection of God's authority. Similarly, Hosea 11:1-4 showcases God's unwavering love despite Israel's spiritual infidelity.

Jesus also addressed this theme in Matthew 21:33-46, where he told the parable of the tenant farmers, emphasizing Israel's stewardship and accountability. These scriptures collectively raise crucial questions: What consequences arise from prioritizing worldly conformity over God's design? How can believers balance cultural engagement with faithfulness to God's distinct plan?

As we reflect on Israel's history and God's instructions, we are reminded that true faithfulness requires surrendering our preferences and practices to align with His divine plan, rather than conforming to the world's standards.

The Israelites' struggle, and ours too, lies in compartmentalizing life into sacred and secular realms. However, Scripture reminds us that everything belongs to God, who created both the physical and spiritual (1 Corinthians 3:23, Psalm 24:1). All aspects of life are interconnected and subject to His sovereignty.

By acknowledging God's ownership and providence, we recognize the importance of adhering to His commands. This perspective is particularly relevant in today's complex world, where issues like climate change and global warming challenge our understanding.

While science provides valuable insights, we must not overlook the divine dimension. Our faith should inform our stewardship of creation and guide our responses to environmental concerns. Recognizing God's sovereignty over all creation (Psalm 24:1) transforms our approach to environmental issues.

By acknowledging His ownership, we are compelled to manage resources wisely, care for the vulnerable, and seek sustainable solutions – not just for scientific or economic reasons, but as an act of worship and obedience.

Obedience is paramount in one's walk of faith. A striking illustration of this principle can be found in 1 Kings 17:3-4, where Elijah receives divine instructions to:

"Go eastward and hide in the Kerith Ravine, east of the Jordan. You will drink from the brook, and I have commanded the ravens to supply you with food there."

Notably, Elijah was directed away from the iconic Jordan River, a site of great spiritual significance, to the seemingly obscure Kerith Ravine. This distinction highlights God's specificity and Elijah's unwavering obedience. After all, the ravens had the Kerith Ravine delivery address, not the Jordan's.

In contrast, Naaman, a Syrian commander, was instructed to dip himself in the Jordan River to cure his leprosy (2 Kings 5:10-14). The difference in locations underscores God's unique plans and purposes for each individual.

The Israelites, too, were called to follow God's distinct calendar and weekly sequence, rather than conforming to the surrounding nations' practices (Exodus 20:8-11, Leviticus 23:1-44). This separation was crucial to maintaining their covenant relationship with God.

Elijah's obedience in going to the Kerith Ravine showcases his trust in God's sovereignty and provision, faith in the specifics of God's instructions, and willingness to separate from worldly influences.

Similarly, believers today are called to obey God's Word, even when it diverges from worldly standards. This obedience demonstrates faith in God's goodness and guidance, leads to experiencing His provision and protection, and maintains their distinct identity as children of God.

Elijah's story teaches that obedience isn't about comparing or compromising with the world; rather, it's about trusting and following God's unique plan.

CHAPTER six

The Evolution of Chronology and Calendars

The harmonization of the Hebrew calendar and dating system with global systems raises fundamental questions. Was this alignment truly driven by cultural, economic, and practical necessities? If so, why did the world's systems evolve without regard for potential discrepancies with God's established order? Conversely, if reverence for God surpassed concerns about inconsistencies, wouldn't people have prioritized adhering to His institutions over theirs?

Two divergent paths emerge: the world's calendars and dating systems underwent significant transformations, yet they remain reluctant to align with God's established order. In fact, Scripture dictates that world calendars should conform to God's calendar, with Abib/Nissan designated as the first month of the year (Exodus 12:2, 13:4).

Interestingly, the current Gregorian calendar has its own inconveniences, often overlooked. For instance: - Seasonal discrepancies: January falls in opposing seasons in the Northern and Southern Hemispheres.

- Geographical anomalies: Crossing the International Date Line allows travelers to celebrate New Year's Day twice, as seen when flying from Auckland, New Zealand to Los Angeles, USA.

- Historical inconsistencies: The Gregorian calendar omitted 10 days in 1582 to align with astronomical observations.

When God instituted the Hebrew calendar, He was aware of these complexities. By establishing a lunar-based calendar tied to agricultural cycles and sacred events, God provided a unique framework for His people.

As we explore the evolution of global systems and their refusal to adapt to God's institutions, we uncover a fascinating paradox. While humanity strives for uniformity and precision, God's calendar stands as a testament to His sovereignty and design.

Despite its historical inaccuracies we discussed previously, Dionysius Exiguus' original calculation remains in use today due to its consistency and practicality. This raises questions about why the Gregorian calendar replaced the Julian calendar, considering the importance of consistency and practicality. We'll explore this further as we continue.

Some speculate that the early church may have deliberately hidden information. Before the BC and AD system, the Jewish people used a calendar, and the Apostles knew the date of the Lord's crucifixion. It's puzzling why Dionysius Exiguus introduced the BC and AD dating system without referencing the existing Jewish calendar or the Julian calendar. However, it's important to note that the Hebrews had a dating system but not a formal calendar during that period.

Let's examine the Julian calendar, introduced by Julius Caesar in 45 BCE. It remained the standard calendar in the Roman Empire and later in Europe for over 1,500 years. Understanding the Julian calendar's history and characteristics will provide context for the subsequent introduction of the Gregorian calendar and the motivations behind its adoption.

Before the widespread adoption of the Julian calendar, various civilizations employed their own calendars, each with unique characteristics. The Roman Republican calendar, used in ancient Rome from 753 BCE to 45 BCE, had 10 months, starting with March (Martius) as the first month.

The Roman Republican calendar later evolved into the Roman Imperial calendar, introduced by Julius Caesar, which added January and February to the beginning of the year, creating the 12-month system we recognize today.

The Roman Republican calendar and the Julian calendar did not coexist as separate calendars. Rather, the Julian calendar replaced the Roman Republican calendar, incorporating its months and festivals, but with the added months of January and February.

The Julian calendar was also known as the Roman Imperial calendar. It became the official calendar of the Roman Empire, and it was used throughout the empire for administrative, civil, and religious purposes.

The terms "Julian calendar" and "Roman Imperial calendar" are often used interchangeably to refer to this calendar system. The Julian calendar remained the standard calendar in the Roman Empire and later in Europe for many centuries, until it was refined into the Gregorian calendar in 1582 CE.

Earlier, there was the Egyptian calendar, used around 3000 BCE, which consisted of 12 months, each with 30 days, plus an additional five days at the end of the year. Its simplicity and consistency made it a useful tool for agricultural and administrative purposes. In contrast, the Babylonian calendar, used around 1800 BCE, employed a lunisolar system, featuring months alternating between 29 and 30 days, reflecting the lunar cycle's influence on timekeeping.

The Greek calendar, used from around the 8th century BCE, varied across city-states, but typically consisted of 12 months, with some months having 29 or 30 days. This diversity reflects the decentralized nature of ancient Greece. The Mayan calendar, used from around 2000 BCE, was a Mesoamerican system that utilized interlocking cycles to measure time, including the Tzolkin (a 260-day cycle) and the Haab (a 365-day solar year).

The Chinese calendar, used from around the 14th century BCE, is a lunisolar calendar with a complex system of cycles, still used today for traditional purposes, such as determining Chinese New Year and auspicious dates. These calendars demonstrate the diverse ways ancient cultures approached timekeeping, with varying starting points, month lengths, and leap year rules. Each system reflects the unique astronomical observations, agricultural cycles, and cultural practices of its respective civilization.

The Julian calendar, introduced by Julius Caesar in 45 BCE, did not have a built-in dating system. Instead, it was a solar-based calendar that divided the year into 12 months. Before the introduction of the Anno Domini (AD) era, various dating systems were used in conjunction with the Julian calendar.

One such system was the Ab Urbe Condita (AUC), which counted years from the founding of Rome in 753 BCE. This system was widely used in ancient Rome and emphasized the city's rich history. Another system was the Olympiad dating system, which used the four-year cycles of the ancient Olympic Games to count years. This system was popular in ancient Greece and highlighted the importance of the Olympic Games.

The Roman consular dating system identified years by the names of the consuls who held office during that year. This system was used for administrative and official purposes, as it provided a clear record of who was in power at a given time. The Regnal years dating system counted years from the accession of a monarch or emperor, emphasizing the ruler's authority and reign.

The introduction of the Anno Domini (AD) era by Dionysius Exiguus in 525 CE revolutionized the way years were numbered. Initially, the system counted from the birth of Jesus Christ, which was designated as 1 AD. However, later scholars, such as the Venerable Bede, detected a flaw in the calculation of Jesus' birthdate. Despite this error, the Anno Domini system became the standard for numbering years in the Julian calendar and its successors, including the Gregorian calendar.

The adoption of the Anno Domini era provided a unified and consistent way to number years, facilitating international communication, trade, and historical record-keeping. Its influence can still be seen today, as the Gregorian calendar, which refined the Julian calendar's leap year rules, remains the widely accepted standard for civil calendars around the world.

The Gregorian calendar, introduced by Pope Gregory XIII in 1582, was not a completely new calendar but rather a refined version of the Julian calendar. The Julian calendar had a small discrepancy in its leap year rule, which added up to a difference of about 11 minutes per year. This may seem insignificant, but over centuries, it added up, and by the 16th century, the calendar had drifted by 10 days from the astronomical seasons.

The Gregorian calendar refined the leap year rule to account for this discrepancy, omitting 10 days from the month of October in 1582 to realign the calendar with the astronomical seasons. However, the adoption of the Gregorian calendar did not happen overnight. Different countries and regions adopted it at various times, with some Eastern Orthodox churches still using the Julian calendar today.

The transition to the Gregorian calendar occurred gradually over several centuries. Spain, Portugal, and Italy were among the first to adopt the new calendar in 1582, followed by Germany and Holland in 1610. Great Britain and its colonies, including what is now the United States, adopted the Gregorian calendar in 1752, omitting 11 days from September. Japan adopted the Gregorian calendar in 1873, Russia in 1918 after the October Revolution, and Greece in 1924.

The Julian calendar was not exactly "inverted" but rather refined and replaced by the Gregorian calendar. The transition was a gradual process that spanned several centuries, with different regions adopting the new calendar at various times. Today, the Gregorian calendar is widely used across the world, although some Eastern Orthodox churches still maintain the traditional Julian calendar.

The omission of 10 days in 1582, which marked the introduction of the Gregorian calendar, did not disrupt the calculation of days such as the weekly Sabbath and other lunar month-based holy days. In the Julian calendar, some days were calculated based on the calendar date, whereas others, like the high day Sabbaths, were determined by the lunar cycle. By omitting 10 days, the Gregorian calendar effectively moved the calendar-based days forward by 10 days, but the days of the week remained the same. For instance, if October 12 was a Friday in the Julian calendar, it became October 22 in the Gregorian calendar, but it was still a Friday. This 10-day shift only affected the dates, not the days of the week, ensuring that the weekly cycle of Sunday to Saturday remained uninterrupted.

To maintain continuity, the Catholic Church and other Christian denominations adjusted the calculation of holy days tied to specific calendar dates, such as Christmas. However, some Eastern Orthodox churches, which continued to use the Julian calendar, did not make this adjustment, resulting in a difference in the calculation of dated holy days compared to Western Christian traditions.

The change also impacted the observance of daily prayers, liturgical readings, and other religious practices tied to specific calendar dates. To accommodate the change, religious authorities had to revise liturgical calendars, prayer books, and other resources to ensure continuity and consistency in worship practices. In contrast, lunar-connected holy days, such as Jewish holy days and the high day Sabbaths, were not affected by the calendar change, as they are determined by the lunar cycle rather than the solar calendar. This highlights the distinction between calendar-based and lunar-based religious practices, which were impacted differently by the introduction of the Gregorian calendar. The weekly Sabbath was also not affected, because the weekly days sequence was not affected.

The Jewish holy days remained unaffected by the omission of 10 days in October since the Jewish calendar, also known as the Hebrew calendar, predates the Julian calendar. Nevertheless, synchronizing the dates between the two calendars posed challenges due to various reasons, including differences in leap year rules, month lengths, and starting points. The Jewish calendar is a lunisolar calendar, based on the cycles of the moon and the sun, whereas the Julian calendar is a solar calendar, based solely on the Earth's orbit around the sun. This difference in calendar systems made synchronization difficult.

Additionally, the Jewish calendar has a complex leap year system to keep it in sync with the solar year, while the Julian calendar has a simpler leap year rule. The starting points of the two calendars also differ, with the Jewish calendar beginning from the creation of the world (Anno Mundi), and the Julian calendar starting from the founding of Rome (Ab Urbe Condita) or later, from the birth of Jesus Christ (Anno Domini).

Cultural and religious differences also played a role, as the Jewish calendar was closely tied to Jewish religious practices and traditions, while the Julian calendar was used for Roman administrative and civil purposes. Furthermore, synchronizing the calendars would have required significant changes to both systems, which might have been impractical for everyday use.

Despite these challenges, early Christian scholars like Eusebius and Jerome attempted to correlate the Jewish calendar with the Julian calendar. However, a direct synchronization of the two calendars was not achieved until much later, with the development of modern chronological systems.

The Hebrew dating system, rooted in ancient Jewish tradition, counts years since creation (Anno Mundi). This system has its origins in the biblical account of creation, where the ages of patriarchs and kings are meticulously recorded, allowing for a continuous count of years. However, the modern Hebrew calendar, used today, was formalized around the 4th century CE, and it counts years from creation, which is calculated to have occurred in 3761 BCE.

During this formalization process, the Hebrew calendar was synchronized with the Julian and Gregorian calendars, adopting the proper year numbering in its Anno Mundi dating system. This synchronization was necessary to ensure consistency and accuracy in dating.

Despite this difference, the modern Hebrew calendar remains deeply rooted in Jewish tradition and continues to play a vital role in Jewish religious and cultural practices. Its formalization and synchronization with other calendars have ensured its continued relevance and accuracy, while also preserving its connection to the rich history and heritage of the Jewish people.

In the 10th century CE, the Hebrew calendar was refined with the introduction of the molad system, which calculates the lunar months and determines the start of each month. This refinement helped to establish a more accurate and consistent calendar.

The Hebrew calendar was first printed in the 16th century CE, making it more widely available and contributing to its standardization.

In the 18th century CE, the Hebrew calendar was synchronized with the Julian calendar, allowing for easier conversion between the two systems. This synchronization facilitated interactions between Jewish communities and the broader world.

Finally, in the 20th century CE, the Hebrew calendar was synchronized with the Gregorian calendar, which is the civil calendar used internationally today. This synchronization has enabled modern Jewish communities to easily coordinate their religious and cultural practices with the global calendar.

Note that the Hebrew calendar has undergone several changes and refinements throughout history, but its core structure has remained relatively consistent. The synchronization with the Julian and Gregorian calendars was a gradual process, with various Jewish communities adopting different conversion methods over time. Today, the Hebrew calendar is used in conjunction with the Gregorian calendar for civil purposes.

There are several instances where historical inaccuracies or outdated practices have been maintained for the sake of consistency and practicality.

The United States continues to use the Imperial system of measurements, such as inches, feet, and pounds, despite the global adoption of the metric system. This is largely due to the practicality of maintaining consistency in commerce, industry, and daily life. The United States continues to use the Imperial system of measurements, such as inches, feet, and pounds, despite the global adoption of the metric system. This is largely due to the practicality of maintaining consistency in commerce, industry, and daily life.

Similarly, the Israelites would have benefited from maintaining their God-given calendar year and its unique weekly sequence, reset with the providential provision of manna.

The QWERTY keyboard layout was designed in the 19th century to prevent typewriter jams by spacing out commonly used letters. Despite the advent of modern keyboards and alternative layouts like Dvorak, QWERTY remains the standard due to widespread familiarity and the impracticality of retraining users.

Daylight Saving Time was originally introduced to save energy during World War I and is still observed in many countries, despite mixed evidence about its current benefits. The practice continues largely for the sake of consistency and tradition.

Many historical names and terms remain in use even if they are based on outdated or inaccurate information. For example, the term "Indians" for Native Americans originated from Christopher Columbus's mistaken belief that he had reached India. Despite its inaccuracy, the term is still widely used. These examples illustrate how certain practices and systems persist due to the challenges and disruptions that would arise from changing them.

Similarly, the calendar system established by Dionysius Exiguus, which places the birth of Jesus Christ at 1 AD, has been preserved to prevent confusion and ensure continuity. Altering the calendar to conform to the more accurate historical estimate of Jesus' birth around 6 BC would have caused substantial disruption. The Anno Domini (AD) system gained widespread acceptance in Europe and eventually globally, forming the foundation of the Gregorian calendar, the most widely used calendar today. Realigning the starting point of the calendar would have necessitated recalibrating all historical dates, a highly impractical task. Consequently, despite the historical inaccuracy, Dionysius Exiguus' original calculation remains in use for the sake of consistency and practicality. This decision prioritizes continuity and stability over absolute accuracy, allowing the calendar to maintain its function as a unified system for tracking time.

Although the Gregorian calendar is the most precise calendar in use today, it contains a 6-year error due to the uncorrected BC/AD dating system. This discrepancy arises from the fact that Jesus Christ's birth is now believed to have occurred in 6 BC, rather than 1 CE. Consequently, the year 2024 AD or CE actually corresponds to 2030 years after Jesus' birth, rather than 2024. Furthermore, the calculated year of creation, 3761 BCE, also contains a 6-year error. It is puzzling that, despite the emphasis on consistency and practicality in maintaining the current calendar system, there is no widespread public awareness of this discrepancy, unlike other acknowledged variations, such as the difference between true north, grid north, and magnetic north. This lack of transparency raises questions about the motivations behind preserving the status quo.

Despite this, a key question lingers: Would it not have been beneficial for the Israelites to preserve their divinely ordained calendar year and unique weekly cycle, initially aligned with the miraculous manna provision? Did God not deliberately disrupt their calendar and establish the seventh-day Sabbath, mirroring the manna pattern?

Embracing obedience to God's commands has the power to unlock life-changing breakthroughs, unleashing transformative discoveries that accelerate positivity and boost humanity's well-being.

Recent discoveries continue to unveil the intricacies of God's creation. In October 2024 CE, news reported a fascinating finding: monotonous noise stimulates a type of fungus that enhances plant growth. This phenomenon, present since creation, has only now been uncovered in the 21st century.

This breakthrough highlights the vast ocean of undiscovered wonders waiting to be explored. For centuries, faithful individuals have tapped into the secrets of nature by following God's orders and commands, achieving remarkable outcomes that science has yet to fully comprehend.

The biblical account of creation (Genesis 1-2) reveals God's intricate design, where every element works in harmony. The seventh day, a day of rest, exemplifies this balance. As God rested, He cultivated peace, joy, and happiness, establishing a rhythm of rest and rejuvenation.

This divine blueprint has inspired countless innovators and scientists throughout history. By embracing God's principles, they've unlocked nature's secrets, discovering the transformative power of prayer and meditation to accelerate healing, gratitude and positivity to boost well-being, community and relationships to foster resilience, and stewardship and care for the environment.

The intersection of faith and science continues to reveal the awe-inspiring complexity of God's creation. As we explore and discover, we're reminded that God's wisdom far precedes human understanding. Nature's secrets await our exploration, inviting us to uncover the hidden wonders of the universe.

Through our journey of discovery, we find that obedience to God's commands can unlock breakthroughs, leading to profound insights and innovations. Moreover, harmony with creation fosters growth and flourishing, reflecting the beauty of God's original design.

In this sacred dance between faith and science, we uncover the depths of God's wisdom, illuminating the path to a brighter future.

In the words of Psalm 19:1, "The heavens declare the glory of God; the skies proclaim the work of His hands." As we continue to unravel the mysteries of creation, may we remain humbled by the vastness of God's design and inspired by the secrets waiting to be uncovered.

The Israelites would have greatly benefited from preserving their divinely ordained calendar year and unique weekly cycle, originally synchronized with the miraculous manna provision. Unfortunately, they chose to conform their God-given calendar, weekly sequence, and other sacred institutions to the ways of the world.

By aligning themselves with worldly rhythms, the Israelites risked losing the distinctiveness of their sacred heritage. Their divinely appointed calendar, infused with spiritual significance, was meant to guide their lives and set them apart as a chosen people.

In adhering to their divinely ordained calendar, the Israelites would have stood as a testament to God's sovereignty and wisdom, shining as a beacon of distinction in a world governed by human norms.

This is why Jesus Christ clashed with the Pharisees and Scribes, who had drifted from God's teachings to pursue their own ideologies, masquerading them as divine principles. They prioritized human traditions over God's commandments, prompting Jesus' stern rebuke (Mark 7:8; Matthew 15:3-9; Luke 11:46).

CHAPTER seven

Hebrew Calendar Reset

Does God ever act without purpose? Isaiah 40:21-28 poses profound questions, challenging our understanding:

Have you not known? Have you not heard? Has it not been told you from the beginning? Have you not understood from the foundations of the earth?' (Isaiah 40:21)

These verses emphasize God's intentional design and infinite wisdom. As the Eternal Lord and Creator of the universe, He never grows weary or faint (Isaiah 40:28). His wisdom transcends human comprehension.

This truth is exemplified in Exodus 12 and 16, where God intentionally disrupted the calendar and sequence of weekdays. This was no impulsive act, but a deliberate and purposeful design, deserving of our adherence and reverence.

God's actions are never arbitrary or without meaning. Every disruption, every change, and every command serves a greater purpose, reflecting His sovereign plan.

Adjusting calendars is not solely a human concern; it also holds spiritual significance. A fascinating example can be found in the biblical account of the Exodus, where God intentionally disrupted the existing calendar cycle.

In Exodus 12:2, God instructs Moses to designate the seventh month, Nisan (or Abib), as the new first month for the Israelites, effectively resetting their calendar year. This sudden change occurred while the Israelites were still in Egypt, and it raises intriguing questions.

Why did God choose to initiate the Passover and Exodus during the seventh month, rather than waiting for the start of the traditional new year? Did this abrupt shift cause inconvenience and disruption to the existing calendar cycle?

The affected year, having only completed six months, was essentially restarted. This divine intervention underscores the importance of aligning timekeeping with God's purposes.

God's decision to reconfigure the Israelites' calendar demonstrates that spiritual significance can supersede practical considerations. If God Himself didn't prioritize consistency and practicality in this instance, why should humans justify maintaining an error in the BC/AD dating system solely for those reasons?

This biblical precedent highlights the value of accuracy and divine alignment in timekeeping, encouraging us to reevaluate our priorities when addressing calendar discrepancies. By examining God's actions in the Exodus narrative, we gain insight into the spiritual dimension of calendars and the importance of synchronizing human systems with divine intent.

Although the Bible doesn't explicitly mention the calendar used before Exodus 12:2, scholarly theories suggest that Tishrei (Ethanim) was the first month before Abib (Nisan) was designated as the new first month. This hypothesis is supported by the cultural exchanges that occurred during the Israelites' sojourn in various regions, starting from Abram's call in Mesopotamia.

It's plausible that the Israelites adopted Tishrei as their first month due to their exposure to neighboring civilizations. However, it's also possible that God didn't introduce a new beginning of the year but rather corrected the Israelites' error, reverting them to the original start of the year that they may have lost during their time in Egypt.

Interestingly, the Babylonians, one of the earliest civilizations, considered Nisanu (similar to Nisan/Abib) as their first month, suggesting that they may have retained the original calendar year. Despite these theories, it's clear that God had specific reasons for adjusting the Hebrew calendar to begin in Abib.

The exact motivations behind God's declaration are secondary to the fact that He intentionally changed the calendar. This divine intervention highlights the importance of aligning timekeeping with God's purposes and will. By examining the historical context and biblical account, we gain insight into the significance of calendars and the value of accuracy in our understanding of time.

Prior to Exodus 12:2, the Hebrew calendar had Tishrei (also known as Ethanim) as its first month. The subsequent months followed in this order: Marheshvan (second), Kislev (third), Tevet (fourth), Shevat (fifth), Adar (sixth), Abib (seventh), Ziv (eighth), Sivan (ninth), Tammuz (tenth), Av (eleventh), and Elul (twelfth).

However, with the instruction given in Exodus 12:2, Abib (also known as Nisan) became the first month of the sacred or religious calendar. This change resulted in a revised order: Abib (first), Ziv (second), Sivan (third), Tammuz (fourth), Av (fifth), Elul (sixth), Tishrei (seventh), Marheshvan (eighth), Kislev (ninth), Tevet (tenth), Shevat (eleventh), and Adar (twelfth).

Notably, the months themselves remained unchanged; only their sequence and the designation of the first month were altered. The calendar currently in use is the civil calendar, which was originally the general calendar before the establishment of the sacred or religious calendar.

The shift in the calendar year, where Tishrei and Abib exchanged positions from first to seventh and vice versa, holds a profound mystery. This alteration undoubtedly carried significant meaning, although the exact interpretation remains unclear. Another intriguing aspect is the replacement of the five months between Tishrei and Abib in the original calendar with a different set of five months in the new calendar year. This swap may symbolize the concept of 'the first shall be last,' (Matthew 19:30, Mark 10:31), but its true significance remains uncertain. Moreover, it may hold prophetic or symbolic significance, awaiting deciphering.

This enigmatic element serves as a reminder of the complexity and depth of biblical teachings, encouraging us to continue exploring and seeking wisdom.

In the present civil calendar, the order begins with Tishrei, followed by Marheshvan (also known as Cheshvan), Kislev, Tevet, Shevat, Adar, Nisan, Iyar, Sivan, Tammuz, Av, and Elul. Interestingly, this means that Passover, which is commanded to be observed in the first month according to Exodus 12:2, actually falls in the seventh month (Nisan) of the civil calendar.

This distinction highlights the coexistence of two calendars in Jewish tradition: the sacred or religious calendar, which begins with Nisan, and the civil calendar, which starts with Tishrei. Both calendars play important roles in Jewish life and observance.

Yes, in ancient Israel, there were two concurrent calendar systems: the civil year and the ritual or sacred year. These two calendar years served different purposes and had distinct starting points.

The civil year, used for administrative and agricultural purposes, began in the autumn, around September or October. This is inferred from Exodus 23:16 and Exodus 34:22, which mention the "feast of ingathering" as occurring at the end of the year. This feast celebrated the harvest season, which typically took place in the autumn.

In contrast, the ritual or sacred year, used for religious and liturgical purposes, began in the spring, around March or April (Abib). However, the Sabbatic year, a crucial aspect of the ritual calendar, commenced in the 7th month of the sacred year, as stated in Leviticus 25:9. This corresponds to September or October in the modern calendar. This implies that both the civil and sabbatical years begin in the seventh month (Tishrei).

The Sabbatic year, also known as the Shmita, was a sabbatical year observed every seventh year, during which the land was to remain uncultivated, and all debts were to be forgiven (Leviticus 25:1-7). The start of the Sabbatic year in the 7th month of the sacred year highlights the importance of synchronizing the ritual calendar with the agricultural cycle.

The coexistence of these two calendar systems allowed the ancient Israelites to manage their civil and religious affairs separately, ensuring that their agricultural and liturgical practices remained aligned with the natural cycles and sacred traditions.

The key consideration is whether the sacred weekly sequence was distinguished from the prevailing sequence used by surrounding cultures.

Although the Bible omits explicit references to observing weekdays, including the seventh day, before the Exodus, let's hypothesize that this silence is due to incidental oversight rather than intentional omission. This assumption posits that both the weekly cycle and Sabbath observance were maintained since the post-flood era, despite the lack of direct scriptural evidence.

In this context, let's revisit the process of counting days to identify the seventh day as the weekly Sabbath. While the Bible doesn't offer explicit guidance on whether the Israelites restarted their weekly count after their time in Egypt, there are several key points to consider.

The biblical account emphasizes the importance of the seventh day as a Sabbath, regardless of whether the count began anew or continued from the pre-Egyptian period.

It's plausible that, just as God interrupted the traditional calendar year in Exodus 12 through the Passover, He also disrupted the weekly cycle in Exodus 16 by providing manna.

In Exodus 12, God reset the calendar, establishing Nisan as the first month (Exodus 12:2). Similarly, in Exodus 16, God may have reoriented the weekly sequence, distinguishing Israel's sacred rhythm from the surrounding nations. Although not explicitly stated, the biblical context suggests that the Passover instructions reset the annual calendar, establishing the month of Abib/Nisan as the first month. Similarly, the manna instructions implicitly reset the weekly cycle, defining the Sabbath as the seventh day.

This intentional disruption would have served as a reminder of God's sovereignty and Israel's unique covenant relationship. By separating their weekly cycle from the prevailing pattern, Israel would have maintained a distinct sacred rhythm, honoring God's design.

If God could reset or restart the Hebrew calendar from any month other than the original first month, designating 1 Abib as the new beginning, couldn't He also initiate a new weekly cycle by sending manna on any day of the original week, making that day the first day of the new week? Parallel to resetting the calendar's start with the Exodus, God may have also redefined the weekly cycle, utilizing the manna as a symbol of His providential care and the Sabbath's institution.

This idea resonates with Scripture, underscoring God's authority to initiate, redefine, and orchestrate the sacred rhythms and cycles that shape the lives of His people.

Regardless of whether the Sabbath was observed before the Exodus or initiated at that time, the manna provision served as a pivotal moment, either re-establishing or establishing the Sabbath. Human nature tends towards forgetfulness, causing customs and traditions to fade over time, especially when replaced by new practices.

The distinction between clean and unclean animals is a good example of forgotten traditions that needed reminding in the days of Moses. Noah knew about clean and unclean animals (Genesis 7:2), which indicates that this knowledge existed long before the laws were given to Moses. However, over the centuries and especially during periods of oppression and cultural assimilation, such knowledge could have been lost or obscured.

The Israelites' long period of slavery in Egypt likely disrupted their ability to maintain and pass down their traditions accurately. The harsh conditions and forced labor would have made it difficult to observe religious practices consistently.

The scriptures suggest that the Israelites needed reminders and restorations of their faith, including the Sabbath. This theme is echoed in various biblical accounts, such as Nehemiah 13:19, where the prophet Nehemiah had to re-establish the Sabbath observance among the post-exilic community.

The Israelites' forgetfulness serves as a cautionary tale, highlighting the importance of remembering and honoring God's works, covenant, and commandments, including the Sabbath.

The Israelites were in exile in Babylon for about 70 years. This period of exile began with the Babylonian conquest of Judah and the destruction of the Temple in Jerusalem around 586 BCE. The return from exile began around 538 BCE when King Cyrus of Persia issued a decree allowing the Jews to return to their homeland and rebuild the Temple.

The account in Ezra describes the efforts to rebuild the Temple and re-establish religious practices, including the celebration of the Passover, after this long period of displacement. This return and restoration were significant for the Israelites as they sought to reconnect with their faith and traditions.

Elsewhere, the Bible does mention the re-establishment of the Passover after it had been neglected, particularly due to the exile. One notable instance is found in the Book of Ezra. After the return from the Babylonian exile, the Israelites celebrated the Passover. Ezra 6:19 states:

"On the fourteenth day of the first month, the exiles celebrated the Passover".

This celebration marked a significant moment of renewal and restoration for the Israelites, reconnecting them with their traditions and heritage after a period of displacement.

To reiterate, the severe oppression the Israelites faced in Egypt likely disrupted their religious observances, including the Sabbath. The Bible highlights the significant hardships they endured, especially under the Pharaoh who didn't recognize Joseph's legacy (Exodus 1:8). This period of intense persecution probably made it challenging for them to maintain their religious practices.

Following their liberation from Egypt, the Israelites struggled with spiritual amnesia, frequently forgetting God's remarkable interventions and their miraculous deliverance from bondage. This tendency to forget God's mighty works and their own history of salvation would become a recurring theme throughout their journey, highlighting the need for reminders and restorations of their faith. Psalm 106:21 laments, "They forgot God their Savior, who had done great things in Egypt," highlighting their tendency to overlook God's interventions in their lives. Similarly, Psalm 78:11 states, "They forgot his works and the wonders that he had shown them," underscoring the Israelites' propensity for spiritual amnesia.

These verses, written centuries after the Exodus, demonstrate a recurring pattern in the Israelites' history - a quickness to forget God's deeds and works. Considering the Israelites' lapse in observing the Passover after just 70 years in exile, it's likely that their cultural and spiritual traditions were significantly eroded during their prolonged 300-year enslavement in Egypt.

This forgetfulness was likely exacerbated by their immersion in Egyptian culture and the absence of a formal religious structure. The Sabbath, a crucial aspect of their covenant with God, may have been neglected or lost amidst the hardships and assimilation.

Although plausible, this idea remains an inference, since Scripture provides no explicit evidence of Sabbath awareness or observance before the Exodus. As mentioned earlier, from either perspective - whether the Sabbath existed pre-Exodus or began then - the manna miracle marked a critical turning point, reaffirming or introducing the Sabbath.

Through this innovative approach, God achieved a multifaceted restoration. He revitalized the Israelites' understanding of the Sabbath, transforming it from an abstract divine concept into a tangible, lived experience. This renewal served as a poignant reminder of their sacred heritage, reconnecting them with their covenant obligations. Ultimately, God's provision of manna reaffirmed His presence in their lives, nurturing a deeper sense of relationship and community.

By withholding manna on the seventh day, God gently reinstated Sabbath observance, distinguishing it from their previous experiences. This renewal emphasized their unique covenant obligations, reorienting the Israelites toward their sacred rhythm.

God's provision of manna reset the weekly cycle, reintroducing the count of weekdays to the Israelites. This implies a prior disruption or loss of their rhythmic observance. Notably, Exodus 16:26 records God's indirect reference to the seventh day, saying only that manna would cease on that day. This subtle language implies a fresh start, with the Israelites receiving a revised weekly sequence.

Furthermore, God remains unchanging, yet He can alter circumstances. This paradox underscores His sovereignty and creative power. While God's nature and character remain constant, His methods and actions can adapt to achieve His purposes.

Some possible reasons God might disrupt the weekday sequence include: Emphasizing the Sabbath's significance. Highlighting its role in Israel's covenant obligations. Reinforcing God's rest after creation.

Disrupting the sequence would distinguish Israel's calendar from surrounding nations', underscoring their unique covenant relationship with God. When God created the world, He had all races in mind, yet chose Israel as a unique people for His purpose and will. They were to be a peculiar people, culminating as His children through Jesus Christ, God incarnate.

Altering the sequence might also foreshadow messianic events or typological fulfillments, such as Jesus' resurrection on the first day of the week. Changing the sequence could symbolize a new covenant era, marking a fresh start for Israel and reinforcing God's ongoing relationship with His people. Furthermore, disrupting the sequence would demonstrate God's authority over time itself, emphasizing His sovereignty and ability to transcend human constructs.

Later on, the giving of the Law at Mount Sinai was not just a reminder but also a formal codification of God's commandments. This was necessary to ensure that the Israelites had a clear, written record of their laws and practices, which could be preserved and followed more reliably.

And so, the re-establishment of laws and practices after the Exodus can be seen as a renewal of the covenant between God and the Israelites. This renewal was essential for re-establishing their identity as God's chosen people and setting them apart from other nations.

The detailed instructions given in Leviticus and other books of the Torah served to educate and guide the Israelites in living according to God's will. These instructions covered various aspects of daily life, worship, and community relations, ensuring that the Israelites could live in a way that was pleasing to God.

The process of re-establishing these laws and practices was crucial for the Israelites to regain their religious identity and maintain their covenant relationship with God. And in this chapter, God initially commands the Israelites to observe the seventh day as the Sabbath, for in the seventh day God rested in his work, and blessed it as holy. And since the manna Sabbath is not mentioned separately as high days are, this implies it was the same seventh day mentioned in the Ten Commandments, further implying the restart in the counting of the seven days of the week, if we come back to the Jewish sacred calendar.

However, the first week of creation, the Genesis of weeks, holds profound significance, which God may disrupt only for a greater purpose, such as "Unless a person is born again, they cannot see the kingdom of heaven."

Although a person's inherent humanity remains unchanged from birth, Christ teaches that spiritual renewal requires being 'born again.' Likewise, the initial sequence of days had its origins in creation, but the reestablished sequence takes on greater depth and significance.

The seven-day pattern established in Genesis 1-2:3 serves as a microcosm of God's eternal plan, reflecting His divine order and purpose. This creation week implies predestination, with each day building upon the previous, culminating in the Sabbath's rest, foreshadowing the real Sabbath mentioned in Hebrews 4.

The Genesis week provides a template for understanding time, space, and human existence within God's created order. It establishes a covenantal framework, with the Sabbath serving as a sign of God's covenant with humanity. The Genesis week also contains eschatological seeds, foreshadowing ultimate redemption and rest in eternity. In the context of Bereshith (Genesis 1-2:3), the blueprint of eternity is set. God initiates creation, establishing the pattern for human existence.

The creation narrative transforms chaos into order, reflecting God's sovereignty. The Genesis week reveals God's purposeful design, guiding history toward its intended destination. The creation week sanctifies time, imbuing each day with divine significance. Bereshith's blueprint echoes throughout eternity, shaping human understanding of God, time, and existence.

Ultimately, from whichever angle, the Sabbath commandment finds its basis in two distinct yet intertwined traditions. Exodus 20:8-11 focuses on God's Sabbath rest at creation, while Deuteronomy 5:12-15 emphasizes Israel's liberation from bondage and God's covenant loyalty. These dual perspectives reinforce the Sabbath's significance as a cornerstone of Israel's spiritual practice and collective identity.

CHAPTER eight

The Ultimate Sabbath

Let's pause to address the seeming contradiction between Exodus 20:8-11, emphasizing God's Sabbath rest, and Deuteronomy 5:12-15, highlighting Israel's liberation. Although together they offer complementary reasons for Sabbath observance, reinforcing its vital role in Israel's spiritual practice and national identity, we must consider: What explains the differing emphases in these two accounts, and what insights can be gleaned from this divergence?

People's interpretations are shaped by their perspectives and contexts. For instance, the phrase "bread and butter" holds different meanings in commerce (basic necessities) and catering (a specific food combination).

Similarly, Moses' understanding of the Sabbath in the Book of Exodus may have been influenced by his contemporaneous context. Initially, he linked the Sabbath to God's seventh-day rest during creation (Genesis 2:2-3) and the seventh day of manna provision (Exodus 16:22-30).

However, in Deuteronomy, Moses possibly refined his perspective, shifting emphasis from creation to Israel's redemption from slavery. This reinterpretation highlighted the Sabbath as a reminder of God's deliverance, resonating more deeply with Israel's experiences and covenant identity.

This highlights that interpretations naturally evolve as context and perspective change. Biblical narratives reflect the complexities and nuances of human understanding. Moses' accounts, in particular, demonstrate theological growth and a deepening understanding of God's message, tailored to the specific needs and experiences of his audience.

According to Leviticus 11:6 and Deuteronomy 14:7, the rabbit is considered an unclean animal for Israelites because it chews cud but lacks a divided hoof. However, Moses' classification was based on the dietary laws for Israel, distinguishing between clean and unclean animals, rather than providing a scientifically accurate description of rabbit biology.

From a biological perspective, rabbits and hares do not truly chew cud like ruminants (cows, sheep), which have a four-chambered stomach. Instead, they practice a unique process called cecotrophy or refection, where they eat, regurgitate, and re-eat their food.

In this process, rabbits and hares reabsorb nutrients, extract vitamins and minerals, and break down cellulose. When re-ingesting their food, they seem to chew cud, manipulating and crushing the pellets in their mouth before re-swallowing. This behavior optimizes nutrient extraction from plant-based foods.

Moses' interpretation reflected the observable behavior, where rabbits appear to chew cud, even though their digestive process differs from true cud-chewing. This highlights the biblical text's focus on practical distinctions for ancient Israelites, rather than providing a detailed scientific analysis.

Initially, God commanded the Sabbath's observance and sanctity without providing explicit reasons. Moses then framed the rationale around God's seventh-day rest in creation. However, the Sabbath's introduction in Exodus, tied to the manna provision, may have led Moses to later recognize its deeper connection to God's redemptive work and promise of future rest.

This reevaluation is reflected in Deuteronomy, where Moses shifts emphasis from creation to redemption, highlighting the Sabbath as a reminder of Israel's deliverance and a foretaste of their future rest in the Promised Land.

However, the ultimate rest is yet to come as Hebrews chapter 4 clearly states.

Back to our main theme, the Sabbath commandment remains unchanged and its significance is clear. As Lord of the Sabbath, Jesus Christ is its ultimate authority. The Sabbath was established in honor of Him, and we observe it to rest in Him. However, Jesus Himself doesn't rest or observe the Sabbath, just as He doesn't pray though we pray to Him.

This highlights the Sabbath's purpose: it was made for humanity's benefit, not humanity for the Sabbath's sake. Jesus' words, "The Sabbath was made for man, not man for the Sabbath" (Mark 2:27), emphasize its intended role – to provide rest, renewal, and communion with God.

The concept of rest in Hebrews chapter 4 is intricately linked to the Lord of the Sabbath, Jesus Christ, who is the embodiment of rest. This rest is not just a cessation from physical labor but a spiritual rest that comes from trusting in Jesus Christ. He is the head and Lord of the Sabbath, and his reign will bring a thousand years of rest before the Judgment Day.

Interestingly, one Christian denomination's name reflects this eschatological hope: the Seventh-day Adventist Church (SDA). Let's examine the significance of their name and its implications, setting aside their specific doctrines for now.

The name "Seventh-day Adventist" combines two key concepts. "Seventh-day" references the Sabbath, the seventh day of rest and worship, highlighting the importance of observing this biblical command. "Adventist" emphasizes the expectation of Christ's return, derived from the Latin "adventus," meaning "coming."

This name captures the essence of Christian eschatology, emphasizing the connection between Sabbath observance and the eagerly awaited second coming of Jesus Christ.

Our straightforward interpretation of the name "Seventh Day Adventist" is that it represents a group of Christians who observe the seventh day, Saturday, as their Sabbath day of rest and worship, while also anticipating the imminent second coming of Jesus Christ.

This name encapsulates the denomination's fundamental beliefs and practices, grounded in their understanding of biblical teachings. Specifically, "Seventh Day" alludes to Saturday, the seventh day of the week, designated as the Sabbath, according to the interpretation of the biblical manna provision (Exodus 16:23, 26 & 30), as stated in the Ten Commandments. Meanwhile, "Adventist" signifies their conviction that Jesus Christ's return is imminent.

In essence, Seventh Day Adventists believe that Jesus' second coming is near and that they should be prepared to meet Him, underscoring their focus on readiness and expectation.

However, in a broader context, beyond the Seventh Day Adventist denomination, the terms "advent" and "adventist" have specific meanings. "Advent" typically refers to the arrival or coming of a notable person, event, or thing. It also denotes a period of time leading up to a significant event or celebration. In the Christian Catholic tradition, the four Sundays preceding Christmas commemorate the coming of Jesus Christ.

Using the word, we could say, "The advent of technology has revolutionized communication." Similarly, we could say that the advent of winter brings cold weather.

On the other hand, an "adventist" could be someone who believes in or anticipates the coming of a particular event, person, or movement, or a person who advocates for or prepares for a significant change or development. For example: He was an adventist of the new energy source, convinced it would transform the industry. The company's adventist approach to innovation led to groundbreaking discoveries.

In general, both "advent" and "adventist" convey a sense of anticipation, preparation, and expectation for something significant to happen or arrive.

In this context, the name "Seventh Day Adventist" carries profound theological significance. It's essential to note that our focus is solely on the meaning behind their name, without delving into the intricacies of any church denominational doctrines or politics. Occasionally, we may touch on specific issues for clarity, but our primary emphasis remains on understanding the name's theological implications.

The term "Seventh Day Adventist" can indeed be understood in the context of Hebrews 4, which describes the Sabbath rest as a foreshadowing of the ultimate rest that believers will experience in Christ. They can be seen as people who are looking forward to the ultimate rest, the true Sabbath, which is symbolized by the seventh-day Sabbath (Saturday). They believe that the weekly Sabbath points to the future rest that God has promised His people. Hebrews 4:9-10 says, "So then, there remains a Sabbath rest for the people of God, for anyone who enters God's rest also rests from their works, just as God did from his."

By observing the seventh-day Sabbath, Seventh Day Adventists are, in a sense, anticipating and participating in the ultimate rest that is to come. They see themselves as adventists, or people who are looking forward to and preparing for, the ultimate fulfillment of God's promise of rest.

Considering the Jewish people's observance of the Sabbath pointed forward to Jesus Christ, and Hebrews 4 anticipates a future Sabbath rest, Jesus' fulfillment of the law raises questions about the mandatory observance of the Seventh Day Sabbath.

However, the Adventist perspective on this matter offers valuable insight. Similarly, the notion that "all days are important" also holds merit, provided weekly worship continues. As time unfolds and knowledge increases, the full understanding of these truths will become clear. Ultimately, with the progression of time and the advancement of knowledge, all will be revealed.

Returning to our narrative, we previously established that the Sabbath honors the Creator of all things, as stated in John 1:3, who is also the Lord of the Sabbath. This applies to both high-day Sabbaths (Exodus 12:16) and weekly Sabbaths following the provision of sustenance (Exodus 16:25-26). Ultimately, the Sabbath points to the rest provided through Jesus Christ, as explained in Hebrews chapter 4.

However, Judaism and Christianity diverge on the significance of Jesus Christ. In Judaism, observing the seventh-day Sabbath is a mandatory command. In contrast, Christianity, while rooted in Jewish heritage, places unique emphasis on Jesus Christ, leading to varying perspectives on the necessity of specific Sabbath observance.

Jewish perspectives on Jesus vary across different branches, communities, and individuals.

However, in Judaism, Jesus Christ is not considered the Messiah, a central figure, or the Son of God, and his significance is viewed differently than in Christianity. Instead, he is regarded as a Jewish teacher or rabbi. Some Jewish texts, such as the Talmud, mention Jesus (Yeshu), often in a critical or dismissive manner.

In Reform Judaism, Jesus is seen as a moral teacher and a precursor to modern ethical and social justice movements. Liberal Judaism views Jesus as a Jewish prophet and teacher, albeit not divine. Conservative Judaism considers Jesus a Jewish teacher, but his teachings lack authoritative status.

Judaism still awaits the coming of the Messiah, who will fulfill specific prophetic expectations, such as rebuilding the Temple and restoring Jerusalem. Jesus is not considered this Messiah. Nonetheless, Jesus' Jewish roots and teachings are acknowledged. Many Jewish scholars study Jesus' teachings within their historical and cultural context. Judaism shares some texts with Christianity, like the Hebrew Bible.

In this context, Jewish people continue to await the Messiah's arrival, which is why they observe the Sabbath as a sacred reminder of God's covenant. Although they acknowledge the Sabbath as a tribute to the Creator, many do not recognize Jesus Christ as the fulfillment of the Passover's symbolic significance or as the long-awaited Messiah.

However, a smaller group of Jewish disciples of Jesus Christ understood this connection, embracing him as the ultimate Passover Lamb who sacrificed himself for humanity's redemption. These early Jewish followers of Jesus, including apostles like Peter, John, and Paul, played a crucial role in spreading this message, gaining numerous disciples from among both Jewish people and Gentiles.

Unfortunately, the majority of Jewish people during Jesus' time and throughout history have not accepted him as the Messiah foreshadowed by the Exodus' Passover. Despite Old Testament prophecies and Jesus' miracles, his claims of divinity and messianic role were met with skepticism and resistance.

This divide stems from differing interpretations of biblical prophecy and the nature of the Messiah. Jewish tradition anticipates a Messiah who will bring political liberation, restore Jerusalem, and establish a earthly kingdom. In contrast, Christianity views Jesus as the spiritual Messiah who brought salvation and redemption through his sacrifice.

Notable exceptions include Jewish Christians, also known as Messianic Jews, who integrate Jesus' teachings into their Jewish heritage. Organizations like Jews for Jesus and Messianic Jewish Alliance of America represent this growing movement.

Generally, Judaism predominantly adheres to Moses' explanation for observing the Sabbath as outlined in Exodus 20:8-11, which emphasizes God's rest after creation. This perspective tends to overshadow the alternative rationale presented in Deuteronomy 5:12-15, which highlights Israel's deliverance from slavery.

Interestingly, some Christian denominations have also adopted this Exodus-based perspective on Sabbath observance, emphasizing the Sabbath as a commemoration of God's creative rest. In contrast, others prioritize the Deuteronomy account, focusing on the Sabbath as a celebration of Israel's liberation and God's covenant faithfulness.

And so, Within Christian circles, diverse perspectives on the Sabbath exist. Some believers, affirming Jesus Christ as the Passover Lamb and Messiah, question whether the literal Sabbath initiated in Exodus specifically prefigured Him as the ultimate rest.

Biblical connections suggest otherwise. The book of Hebrews links Jesus to the Sabbath rest, indicating that believers enter His rest through faith. Additionally, Colossians views Sabbath observance as a shadow of things to come, with Jesus being the substance. Genesis and Exodus establish the Sabbath as a celebration of God's creative and redemptive work.

The ultimate rest is indeed tied to Jesus' second coming. His resurrection, which occurred on the first day of the week, inaugurated a new era.

Early Christians, following Jewish tradition, initially observed the Sabbath. However, as Christianity spread, Sunday became the day to commemorate Jesus' resurrection.

This shift reflects Jesus' own statements about being Lord of the Sabbath, as well as the apostolic church's focus on Jesus' resurrection and its implications.

The keeping of the Lord's Day until Jesus' return acknowledges His victory over death and sin, and the promise of ultimate rest and redemption.

Before Judgment Day, Jesus will return, bringing the ultimate Sabbath – eternal rest and peace – for believers.

In Christian communities, opinions on the Sabbath's connection to Jesus vary. Despite recognizing Jesus as the Passover Lamb and Messiah, some question whether the Exodus Sabbath specifically foreshadowed Him as the ultimate rest.

Scriptural links suggest a profound connection. Jesus represents the true Sabbath rest, and the Sabbath prefigures Jesus, the substance of redemption.

Jesus' resurrection on the first day of the week launched a new era, shifting the focus from Sabbath observance to celebrating His victory.

By observing the Lord's Day, believers acknowledge Jesus' triumph and anticipate the ultimate Sabbath – eternal rest – at His second coming.

In traditional Judaism, the seventh day of the creation week holds profound significance, but its connection to Jesus Christ and the ultimate Sabbath is not widely acknowledged. However, biblical prophecy suggests a larger narrative, potentially spanning six thousand years from creation to the Sabbath millennium, culminating in Jesus' Second Coming.

According to this interpretation, human history is divided into two distinct periods: six thousand years of labor and struggle, corresponding to the six days of creation, followed by a thousand-year Sabbath of rest and peace, inaugurated by Jesus' return, paralleling the seventh-day rest.

This eschatological perspective, rooted in biblical texts such as Psalm 90:4 and 2 Peter 3:8, views the seventh-day Sabbath as a foreshadowing of the ultimate Sabbath, when God will bring redemption and restoration.

Although this understanding is not mainstream in indigenous ethnic Jewish religion, there are exceptions. Some Jewish believers in Jesus, known as

Messianic Jews, recognize him as the ultimate Sabbath, fulfilling the prophetic significance of the seventh day.

Messianic Jewish groups, such as Jews for Jesus and the Messianic Jewish Alliance of America, represent this growing movement, blending Jewish heritage with Christian faith. These groups emphasize Jesus' fulfillment of Old Testament prophecies and his role as the Messiah, bridging the gap between Jewish and Christian traditions.

In this context, Jesus' teachings and sacrifice are seen as the culmination of God's plan, ushering in a new era of redemption and rest, ultimately leading to the promised Sabbath millennium.

References to relevant biblical texts and Messianic Jewish groups provide additional context and insight into this complex and multifaceted topic.

There are Christians who share similarities with Messianic Jews, blending their Christian faith with Jewish heritage. These individuals, often referred to as Hebrew Roots or Christian Zionists, embrace Jewish traditions and practices.

Some of these Christians observe Passover in accordance with Jewish customs, rather than commemorating it through the Eucharist or Lord's Supper. They also keep the Sabbath, honoring the seventh-day rest as a tribute to God's creation, mirroring Jewish observance.

This perspective has merits, acknowledging the Hebrew roots of Christianity and the significance of God's rest on the seventh day. However, it stops short of recognizing Jesus Christ as the fulfillment of the Passover and the ultimate Sabbath reality.

Although unintentional, this oversight misses the crux of God's redemption plan through Jesus Christ. Jesus' sacrifice and resurrection are the culmination of God's plan, ushering in a new covenant and redefining the significance of Jewish festivals and observances.

Notable groups within this movement include Messianic Gentiles, who adopt Jewish practices while maintaining Christian faith. The Hebrew Roots Movement also plays a significant role, emphasizing Torah observance and Jewish roots. Additionally, Christian Zionists are part of this landscape, actively supporting Israel and exploring connections between Jewish and Christian traditions.

These groups share a common interest in bridging the gap between Judaism and Christianity, with some individuals embracing Jewish customs and practices as a way to deepen their Christian faith.

Key figures like Pastor John Hagee and Rabbi Jonathan Cahn have contributed to this growing interest in Jewish-Christian reconciliation.

While this perspective has value, integrating Jewish heritage with Christian faith, it requires a deeper understanding of Jesus' role in God's redemption plan to fully grasp the ultimate truth.

In accordance with biblical prophecy, specifically Revelation 7:4-8 and 14:1-3, it is believed that Jewish people from all twelve tribes will be reunited and integrated into the universal Body of Christ, also known as the invisible church. This reunification is contingent upon their recognition and acceptance of Jesus Christ as the Messiah, or alternatively, by God's gracious initiative bestowed upon the Chosen People.

As stated in John 14:6, Jesus declares, "No one comes to the Father except through me." This affirmation underscores the central role of Jesus Christ as the sole mediator between God and humanity.

In this eschatological context, the twelve tribes of Israel will be redeemed and grafted back into the olive tree of God's covenant people, as described in Romans 11:11-32. This redemption will fulfill God's promise to Abraham, Isaac, and Jacob, and demonstrate the unity and completeness of the Body of Christ.

The 144,000 sealed from the twelve tribes, mentioned in Revelation 7, represent the number of Jewish believers who will play a pivotal role in God's end-time plan. The sealed select may serve as evangelists, proclaiming the Gospel to all nations and heralding the return of Jesus Christ.

This future reconciliation is rooted in Jesus' prayer for unity in John 17:21-23, where He implores the Father to reunite all believers in Himself. The ultimate goal is for Jewish and Gentile believers to come together as one body, worshipping the Father through Jesus Christ.

Although many Jewish people do not believe Jesus is Lord and Creator of the universe, their status as the Chosen People may still bring salvation to some, for God's call is irrevocable (Romans 11:28-31).

CHAPTER Nine

Biblical Sabbaths: The First and Seventh Days

God's intentional design ensures that every aspect of creation serves a greater plan. The seven-day week holds profound significance, with each day potentially carrying unique meaning and purpose. The seventh day, as Sabbath, foreshadows the millennial reign of Christ and the ultimate rest before eternity. However, what significance do the other six days hold?

The first day of the week holds remarkable importance, particularly given Jesus Christ's resurrection on this day. This event may be linked to the first day of creation, where God separates light from darkness, establishing night and day, in that order (Genesis 1:3-5). Jesus, the Light of the World, rises on the first day, symbolizing the triumph of light over darkness.

This parallel is striking: Jesus is the Firstborn of all creation, and the first day of creation introduces light, paving the way for life. On the fourth day, God creates the sun, moon, and stars, yet Jesus is the ultimate source of light, as stated in Revelation 21:23, "The city has no need of sun or moon, for the glory of God illuminates it, and the Lamb is its lamp."

Jesus' connection to the first day of creation underscores His role as the originator of life (Zoe), and light, bridging old and new creation (John 1:4).

The other days of the week may also hold hidden significance. The second day's separation of waters possibly symbolizes spiritual separation and purification. The third day's emergence of land and vegetation may foreshadow new life and abundance. The fourth day's introduction of celestial bodies could represent divine order and governance. The fifth day's population of oceans and skies highlights God's creative diversity. The sixth day's creation of humanity reflects God's image and purpose.

Unpacking the creation days invites deeper reflection: How do they mirror humanity's journey, and what symbolism lies within God's sequential creative acts?

Ultimately, God's intentional design ensures that every aspect of creation, including the seven-day week, serves a greater purpose, revealing His majesty and plan for humanity.

The birth and death periods of Jesus Christ hold significant importance and should not be overlooked. Just as the dates of Easter are determined by lunar calculations, varying annually between March 22 and April 25, understanding the actual timing of Jesus' birth and death is crucial.

Astronomical and zodiacal influences play a role in individual lives from birth, making timing essential. The ancient Jewish calendar, based on lunar cycles, underscores the connection between celestial events and human experiences.

The Bible, while cautioning against astrology in Isaiah 47:13-14 and Deuteronomy 18:10-14, acknowledges its significance. Astrology's power demands responsible handling, lest it leads to misinformation and harmful decisions.

The Bible warns against misusing astrology, not because it's inherently evil, but because of its potential to distract from God's sovereignty and lead to idolatry.

Understanding the timing of Jesus' birth and death can provide valuable insights: Jesus' birth coincided with the Jewish festival of Sukkot (John 1:14, Leviticus 23:33-43), symbolizing God's dwelling among humanity.

His death and resurrection aligned with Passover (John 19:14, 31-37, Exodus 12:1-28), representing redemption from slavery to sin.

Recognizing these connections deepens our appreciation for Scripture's historical and cultural context.

Exploring the astronomical and zodiacal significance of Jesus' life events can enhance our comprehension of biblical prophecy and symbolism, as well as reveal hidden patterns and meanings within Scripture.

This inquiry can offer profound insights into the biblical narrative, inviting a deeper understanding of God's plan and purposes.

By examining the celestial context surrounding Jesus' birth, life, death, and resurrection, we may uncover: Fresh perspectives on biblical prophecy and its fulfillment.

Deeper connections between Old and New Testament themes.

Increased appreciation for Scripture's rich symbolism and imagery.

A broader understanding of God's sovereignty over time and creation.

Such exploration encourages a holistic approach to Scripture, integrating faith, history, and astronomy to illuminate the remarkable story of Jesus Christ.

By acknowledging the intersection of faith and astronomy, we honor God's intricate design and sovereignty over creation.

This perspective encourages responsible exploration of astrology, avoiding harmful or idolatrous practices while uncovering the rich tapestry of biblical meaning and symbolism.

Although the Bible doesn't specify Jesus' exact birthdate, it offers clues indicating that His birth likely didn't occur in winter (December).

Luke 2:1-4 implies the Roman census would have taken place during a more favorable time, probably spring or fall, when travel was easier and weather conditions were mild. This timeframe aligns with the Jewish festival Sukkot (Feast of Tabernacles), typically occurring in September-October.

The festival holds profound significance in relation to Jesus' birth. This joyous festival's themes remarkably align with the events surrounding Jesus' arrival.

Sukkot represents God dwelling among His people, a promise fulfilled through Jesus' birth, as stated in John 1:14. Jesus, the Light of the World (John 8:12), brought light and salvation to humanity, echoing Sukkot's symbolism of light.

The festival's atmosphere of joy and celebration also resonates with the nativity story. Shepherds tending their flocks by night, as mentioned in Luke 2:8, suggests a warmer season, consistent with Sukkot's autumn timing.

Further evidence supports a non-winter birth. Notably, astronomers have discovered a rare harmonic convergence of celestial bodies occurring in 3-2 BC, visible in the Middle East. This extraordinary event may have heralded Jesus' birth.

However, pinpointing the exact year poses a challenge. Dionysius Exiguus, a 6th-century scholar, calculated Jesus' birth to be around 1 AD. In contrast, Venerable Bede and other historians argue for a birthdate circa 6 BCE.

Despite this discrepancy, ancient Jewish traditions and oral histories consistently place Jesus' birth during the festive season of Sukkot.

The convergence of celestial events, historical records, and cultural traditions underscores the significance of Sukkot in understanding Jesus' birth.

This intriguing intersection of faith, astronomy, and tradition deepens our appreciation for the complex tapestry surrounding Jesus' life and legacy.

While scholars propose various dates, September-October remains a compelling option. This timeframe aligns with the biblical account of the shepherds and census, and coincides with Sukkot's themes of God's presence and light.

The convergence of these historical, cultural, and astronomical factors underscores the significance of Sukkot in understanding Jesus' birth.

While the exact date remains uncertain, exploring these clues deepens our understanding of Jesus' birth and its significance within Jewish tradition and biblical narrative.

While some Christians downplay the significance of Jesus Christ's physical aspects, emphasizing spirituality instead, it's essential to recognize the intrinsic link between the physical and spiritual dimensions of human existence. After all, it's physical humans who sin or live righteously.

The physical body is an integral part of being human, and birth and death are physical milestones. Jesus' birth, like any human's, was a physical event marked by a specific date and location.

In Genesis 2:7, God forms Adam from dust, then breathes life into him, illustrating the simultaneous creation of physical and spiritual aspects. This harmonious union underscores their equal importance.

The biblical account of Jesus' birth highlights the interconnectedness of physical and spiritual realms. The Magi from the East followed a celestial guide to Bethlehem, indicating Jesus' physical arrival was astronomically significant. The Star of Bethlehem's unusual movement, potentially a planetary alignment or comet, signaled the birth of an extraordinary individual.

Jesus' physical birth was not merely a human event but a cosmic phenomenon, demonstrating the convergence of heavenly and earthly realms. This fusion of physical and spiritual dimensions is rooted in biblical teachings.

Psalm 139:13-14 states that God forms the physical body and knits the spiritual soul together. Similarly, 1 Corinthians 6:19-20 declares the body a temple of the Holy Spirit.

Embracing the interconnectedness of Jesus' physical and spiritual aspects enriches our understanding of His life, teachings, and significance.

By acknowledging the physicality of Jesus' birth, we honor the Incarnation – God becoming flesh – and the profound implications of His earthly existence.

This holistic perspective encourages a deeper appreciation for Scripture's accounts of Jesus' life, death, and resurrection, underscoring the inseparable bond between the physical and spiritual dimensions of human experience.

If Jesus' physical birth triggered a cosmic phenomenon, signifying the convergence of heavenly and earthly realms, it's reasonable to assume that this event would also impact world systems. The profound implications of Jesus' birth would likely resonate throughout the natural and spiritual orders.

Astrologers rely on precise birth data – date, time, and location – to create accurate horoscopes. This ancient practice acknowledges the celestial influences shaping human lives. Considering Jesus' birth caused a remarkable celestial event, knowing its date or season could provide valuable insights.

Understanding the planetary alignments and cosmic patterns surrounding Jesus' birth could reveal hidden connections between heavenly and earthly realms. Astrological analysis might shed light on Jesus' life, ministry, and impact on human history. Recognizing the cosmic significance of Jesus' birth could inform predictions about world events, spiritual shifts, and the unfolding of God's plan.

Historical records and biblical accounts offer clues about Jesus' birth. The Star of Bethlehem, mentioned in Matthew 2:1-12, suggests a rare astronomical occurrence. Ancient Jewish traditions and oral histories place Jesus' birth during Sukkot (Feast of Tabernacles). Scholars propose various dates, with September-October being a compelling option.

Exploring the intersection of astrology, biblical prophecy, and Jesus' birth invites fascinating questions. How do celestial events influence human affairs and spiritual dynamics? Can understanding Jesus' birth chart reveal patterns and themes relevant to His life and teachings? Might this knowledge enhance our comprehension of biblical prophecy and its fulfillment?

Delving into these questions encourages a deeper exploration of the intricate relationships between heaven and earth, spirituality and physicality. By examining the cosmic context surrounding Jesus' birth, we may uncover new perspectives on His life, teachings, and enduring impact on human history.

This inquiry underscores the significance of Jesus' birth as a pivotal moment in time, bridging heavenly and earthly realms. Unraveling its mysteries can enrich our understanding of the complex tapestry that is human existence.

Knowing the exact dates or days of the season of Jesus Christ's crucifixion and resurrection is equally significant as understanding His birth. The events surrounding Jesus' birth, such as the Bethlehem Star, demonstrate the importance of celestial alignments in biblical narratives.

The star, likely a comet or planetary alignment, preceded Jesus' birth and moved westward for several days or months before stopping overhead at the location where Jesus lay. This extraordinary phenomenon would have begun shining and moving well before Jesus' birth, allowing the Magi to travel for an extended period.

Similar to the pillar of fire guiding the Israelites during the Exodus, the Magi may have rested when the star stopped overhead or at daybreak. The timing was remarkably synchronized, ensuring the Magi found Jesus at His birthplace.

Jesus' death was accompanied by two remarkable phenomena: a massive earthquake (Matthew 27:51-54) and a total solar eclipse without the moon intervening (Luke 23:44-45). These events underscore the significance of Jesus' birth and death in God's plan.

This trilogy of events – the Bethlehem Star, the earthquake and solar eclipse, and the resurrection – forms an indelible narrative arc. Each moment underscores the others, weaving a tapestry of divine significance.

Through these celestial and terrestrial occurrences, God underscored the importance of Jesus' birth, death, and resurrection.

By acknowledging the importance of Jesus' birth, death, and resurrection, humanity honors God's sovereignty and design.

From another complementary angle, it is essential to understand the timeline of events, especially pivotal moments in history, such as these. Knowing the dates and sequence of these significant events provides valuable context and insight into their impact and significance.

The uncertainty surrounding the exact date of Jesus Christ's birth had devastating consequences. When Herod, driven by a desire to eliminate the newborn King of the Jews, learned of Jesus' birth, he ordered the massacre of all male infants in Bethlehem under the age of two. This tragic event, known as the Massacre of the Innocents, resulted in the loss of countless innocent lives.

If Herod had known the precise date or season of Jesus' birth, the number of victims would have been significantly lower, limited only to those in close proximity to Jesus. However, due to the lack of knowledge, many babies were caught in the crossfire, paying the ultimate price for being born around the same time as the future King.

This event highlights the significance of understanding the timeline of Jesus' life and the importance of accurate knowledge. The lives lost in Bethlehem serve as a poignant reminder of the consequences of uncertainty and the importance of seeking truth.

Overlooking pivotal events like the death and resurrection of Jesus Christ suggests a lack of concern and seriousness about spiritual matters among early church leaders. It's comparable to forgetting one's own birthday or a nation's independence day—such oversights typically result from carelessness, negligence, and a lack of interest.

Alternatively, one might wonder if this omission was a deliberate act by influential individuals opposing Christ, seeking to downplay the significance of these events. Considering the fierce battle between light and darkness, it's a plausible scenario. In the absence of light, darkness prevails, and where knowledge is scarce, foolishness thrives. This underscores the importance of understanding and acknowledging the truth, for it is the light that dispels darkness and fosters wisdom.

The Lord emphatically states that his people perish due to a lack of knowledge (Hosea 4:6). This profound statement prompts introspection: what essential knowledge are we missing? Throughout history, humanity's understanding has evolved, significantly impacting mortality rates.

In ancient times, limited knowledge led to widespread suffering and death from preventable diseases. However, discoveries like vaccinations have revolutionized healthcare, saving countless lives. By introducing tiny, harmless fragments of pathogens, vaccines stimulate our immune system to produce antibodies, safeguarding us against future infections.

This principle raises intriguing questions: if our bodies can be induced to build defenses through vaccines, could the environment similarly respond to intentional actions? Consider climate change, largely caused by human activities. By adjusting our behaviors and timing, can we mitigate its effects?

Perhaps other cosmic phenomena also respond to our actions, location, and timing. Could synchronizing our endeavors with natural rhythms and cycles yield benefits? The world operates as an interconnected ecosystem, where every element influences others.

Ancient cultures recognized this harmony, often aligning their practices with celestial events and seasonal changes. Modern science confirms these instincts, revealing intricate relationships between human activities, environmental factors, and cosmic patterns.

Embracing this holistic understanding can transform our relationship with the environment and universe. By acknowledging the interconnectedness of all things, we can harness the power of knowledge to create a more harmonious, thriving world.

In the timeless wisdom of Proverbs, a profound truth is revealed: "Where there is no vision, the people perish; but he who keeps the law, happy is he" (Proverbs 29:18). This ancient verse speaks to the transformative power of foresight, guidance, and obedience.

Without a clear vision, communities falter and lose direction. Goals and purpose fade, leaving individuals adrift in a sea of uncertainty. However, when a vision is cast, hope revives, and people unite toward a common purpose.

On the other hand, those who embrace and uphold God's laws discover true happiness. This happiness is not merely a feeling but a state of being rooted in obedience, faith, and wisdom. By keeping the law, individuals align themselves with divine principles, cultivating inner peace, joy, and fulfillment.

Vision, knowledge, and obedience are intertwined. A clear vision guides our actions, while obedience to God's laws ensures our steps align with His will. Knowledge provides the know-how to execute this vision.

Ultimately, obedience takes precedence, as we cannot possess all the knowledge and vision God has. Following His commands encompasses all, covering the gaps in our understanding.

The story of creation is a profound mystery. The Bible doesn't reveal why God chose to create the universe in six days, resting on the seventh. With His limitless power, He could have effortlessly created everything in a single day. Yet, He deliberately unfolded His masterpiece over six days, establishing a rhythm that would shape human existence. The Lord didn't explain why He didn't adopt an alternative schedule, such as working three days, pausing, and then completing creation.

Similarly, the Lord didn't disclose why He established a seven-day week, rather than a five-day or eight-day cycle. His silence invites trust, encouraging us to follow His commandments, acknowledging that He knows what's best.

This lack of explanation underscores the importance of faith and obedience, reminding us to rely on God's infinite wisdom and sovereignty.

God's ways defy human logic, and His wisdom transcends our understanding. We're invited to trust His commandments, acknowledging His all-knowing nature. The Sabbath, observed on the seventh day, stands as a testament to God's deliberate design. This day of rest isn't determined by a fixed calendar or arbitrary schedule, but by the simple act of counting – just like the sabbatical year. This emphasizes the importance of obedience and faithfulness, as we align our lives with God's intentional rhythm.

The Bible offers two compelling reasons for observing the Sabbath. In Exodus, we're reminded of God's rest after creation, while Deuteronomy highlights the deliverance of Israel from slavery. These dual perspectives enrich our understanding, revealing the Sabbath as both a celebration of God's creative power and a testament to His liberating love.

Initially, the Ten Commandments were given to the Israelites, who were focused on reaching the Promised Land. However, through Jesus Christ, the promise expands to encompass eternal life. The Sabbath serves as a bridge between creation, deliverance, and redemption – a day to rest, reflect, and rejuvenate our spirits.

Keeping the Sabbath acknowledges God's sovereignty, creative power, and guiding presence in our lives. In this sacred rhythm, we find peace, hope, and purpose – gifts from a loving God who knows best. In the quiet moments of the Sabbath, we're reminded that God's ways are not our ways, but His wisdom is always at work, shaping our lives and our world.

As Christians and Messianic Jews, we prioritize the essential over the peripheral. Jesus Christ, the Lord of the Sabbath, is the central figure we honor. The Sabbath was instituted to commemorate Him, and honoring Him encompasses all aspects of our faith, including the Sabbath.

Just as the commandments and statutes are condensed into two fundamental New Testament principles – loving God with our entire being and loving our neighbors as ourselves – every day, Sabbath, and holy day is transcended by recognizing Jesus Christ as the Lord of Lords and Creator of all.

Through His resurrection on the first day of the week, the church was born, and eternal life became a certainty. This pivotal event redefines our understanding of time and sacred observances, with Jesus Christ at the forefront.

In essence, our devotion to Jesus encompasses every aspect of our faith, integrating the Sabbath, holy days, and daily life into a seamless expression of worship and obedience to Him.

And so, Beyond Good Friday lies the significance of the first day of the week, when God created light, the invisible force enabling visibility of all subsequent creations. On the seventh day, God rested, yet remained active, creating rest, relaxation, joy, and essential necessities for humanity's well-being, including the sanctification of His name.

Jesus Christ, the Alpha and Omega, the beginning and the end, is the Lord of the Sabbath. He is observed during the Unleavened Bread's first and seventh days. Remarkably, Jesus embodies the ultimate Sabbath: His resurrection occurs on the first day, symbolizing new life. His rest on the seventh day represents complete redemption. In Jesus Christ, the Sabbath finds its fulfillment, reconciling apparent discrepancies. He is the harmonious union of creation's beginning and humanity's ultimate rest.

CHAPTER ten

Two Distinct Sabbaths Beyond Good Friday

According to Daniel 12:4 and Revelation 22:10, God foretold a surge in knowledge in the last days, enabling believers to unravel biblical mysteries. Yet, this prophecy also raises essential questions: Aren't our current interpretations limited by early church councils' selective scripture compilation? Don't theological and cultural biases impact our understanding?

Recognizing the historical context and potential limitations, we acknowledge that our comprehension is incomplete and open to growth. Humility allows for ongoing revelation and refinement of truth.

Embracing this mindset, we navigate biblical complexities, welcoming new insights while honoring timeless truths. We uncover Scripture's riches with an open and discerning heart, balancing reverence for the sacred text with openness to the Holy Spirit's ongoing guidance.

This perspective fosters a deeper understanding, unencumbered by dogma and tradition, and invites continuous discovery and spiritual growth.

Earlier, our biblical search yielded no references to the Sabbath before the Exodus era, nor any mention of weekday sequences or identities following the creation week. The Bible's silence on these topics is noteworthy. Interestingly, the non-canonical Book of Jasher (70:41-51), rejected by both Jewish and Christian traditions, provides a contrasting view, suggesting that Moses requested one day of rest per week, thereby implying the Sabbath's existence prior to the Exodus.

However, according to Jasher 70:44, Moses requested a day of rest per week, not specifically the seventh day (Saturday) or the Sabbath. The text does not imply that Moses approached Pharaoh on the seventh day of the creation week, starting the count on Sunday.

In Jasher 70:47, Pharaoh declared the seventh day, counted from his proclamation, as the Israelites' day off. This decree, issued by Pharaoh and Moses (son of Bathia), occurred before God's call to Moses. Notably, Jasher 70:49 attributes this development to God's remembrance of the Israelites, intending to save them for their fathers' sake.

The significance lay in counting, not identifying the original seventh day of creation. Jasher distinguishes between "the seventh day" and "the Sabbath," without mentioning the latter. God may have synchronized this seventh day with the creation week's seventh day, or not. The text emphasizes the importance of counting and obedience, rather than linking it explicitly to the creation week.

This nuanced understanding highlights the distinction between the biblical Sabbath and the seventh day decreed by Pharaoh and Moses, underscoring the complexity of ancient Israelite traditions and the evolution of Sabbath observance.

To reiterate, thee weekly Sabbath, determined by counting, remains distinct. Moses' request wasn't specifically for the seventh day or the Sabbath but for one day of rest per week. This day, by default, becomes the seventh day after commencement.

Interestingly, Sunday, the first day of the week, becomes the seventh day after workdays for many Christians.

Back to the Bible, Genesis records God blessing the seventh day (Genesis 2:3), while Exodus 16 institutes the Sabbath as the seventh day, commemorating the initiation of manna. The Sabbath, part of the Decalogue, held ceremonial significance, alongside sociological and moral value.

Similar to modern sacraments like baptism and the Lord's Communion, the Sabbath served as a physical observance with spiritual implications. However, unlike these New Testament sacraments, which symbolize ongoing spiritual realities, the Sabbath foreshadowed Jesus' gift of rest.

In the New Testament, Jesus' teachings and the apostles' writings reframe the significance of the Sabbath. Jesus declares Himself Lord of the Sabbath (Matthew 12:8), and the Sabbath is fulfilled in Christ (Colossians 2:16-17). Furthermore, the New Covenant emphasizes rest in Christ, as seen in Hebrews 4:9-10.

This nuanced understanding highlights the Sabbath's evolution from a ceremonial observance to a symbol of eternal rest in Jesus Christ.

Did the Sabbath cease with Christ since it was fulfilled in him?

The notion that the Sabbath ceased with Christ's fulfillment is partially accurate, yet it overlooks a crucial distinction: the Sabbath transcends a specific day of the week. The Old Testament foreshadowed the New Testament, and the

New Testament marks the Beginning of the End, echoing Genesis 1:1 and John 1:1, where "Beginning" signifies "Berēshîth."

In this context, Sabbath observance continues, but with renewed understanding, as Jesus Christ is its Lord. While the Israelites sought the Promised Land, Canaan, many still await a political Messiah and New Covenant. However, those who accepted Jesus Christ as Messiah and New Covenant now observe the Sabbath in its true essence.

No longer confined to a specific day, they gather on Sunday, the resurrection day, to break bread, as the earliest church did. The central core of Sabbath observance lies not in uniformity but in honoring its true meaning: resting in Christ, worshiping God, and acknowledging Jesus as Lord of the Sabbath.

What God created on the Sabbath – rest, relaxation, and rejuvenation – remains worthy of praise and worship. Jesus Christ's lordship over the Sabbath transforms its observance, shifting focus from calendar days to spiritual significance, unity, and communion with Him.

In this light, observing the Sabbath on the first day, last day, or any day becomes secondary to embracing its inherent values: communion with God, gratitude, and celebration of Christ's redemption.

Jesus' prophecy for the post-resurrection era hint at Sabbath observance in Matthew 24:20, where He advises praying that flight doesn't occur on a Sabbath or in winter. Notably, Jesus never explicitly linked the seventh or any other day to the Sabbath.

As previously established, the weekly Sabbath fell on the seventh day, later standardized to Saturday for clarity and consistency. Today, we rely on calendars rather than counting. However, Jesus Christ, being Jewish, communicated with his contemporaries in their familiar context.

Notably, Jesus never explicitly stated that the Sabbath was Saturday. Scripture records instances where God disregarded the Israelites' Sabbaths and new moons (as seen in 2 Chronicles 36:21 and Ezekiel 20:39-40). This distinction highlights the difference between the seventh day, a specific calendar day, and the Sabbath, a day of rest, worship, joy, and self-reflection.

God didn't disregard the Israelites' Saturdays or seventh days but rather their sabbaths, which fell on the seventh day of each week or coincided with high holy days.

Jesus Christ's references to the Sabbath emphasized its spiritual significance: a day for rest, worship, joy, self-introspection, and non-violence. He focused on the essence of the Sabbath, rather than solely its calendar designation.

This nuanced understanding highlights the distinction between the Sabbath's calendar placement and its deeper spiritual meaning, which Jesus Christ reaffirmed and reemphasized in his teachings.

The New Testament emphasizes the equality and goodness of all the God-given days (Romans 14:5-6, Galatians 4:9-10, Colossians 2:16-17). However, the pivotal events of Passion Week unfolded on specific dates in the Hebrew calendar, underscoring the significance of sacred time and space.

While the act of praying to God from any location is highly encouraged and important (1 Timothy 2:8), having a dedicated place of worship for communal prayers and reflection, such as a church or temple, can provide a more focused and reverent environment for spiritual reflection and community. These sacred spaces are often designed to enhance the experience of worship and to foster a deeper connection with the divine.

While watching a soccer match on a large screen can offer a clear view and the ability to see replays, experiencing the game in person provides a more immersive and emotional connection to the event. Although you may miss certain events happening behind your grandstand, the sense of being present in the moment and the energy of the crowd can create a more profound connection with the sport.

Similarly, having a designated place of worship holds significance in many religious traditions, providing a sacred space for believers to gather, pray, and engage in spiritual practices together. Throughout history, temples, synagogues, churches, mosques, and other places of worship have served as focal points for communities to express their faith and seek connection with the divine.

Likewise, meeting for worship on the day you are sure is the right day, such as the Sabbath or the Lord's Day, can offer more spiritual uplifting than meeting on a day you doubt its significance. The observance of specific holy days and the recognition of their importance in a faith tradition can help believers deepen their understanding and connection with their religious beliefs. This aligns with the importance of identifying and verifying the Sabbath following the crucifixion, a day of great significance in Jewish tradition that carried profound spiritual meaning.

The act of coming together for worship on these significant days not only strengthens individual faith but also contributes to the collective spiritual bond of a religious community. By honoring and observing these sacred moments, believers can draw inspiration, find solace, and renew their commitment to living out their faith in their daily lives.

The Passion Week, which is narrated in the Gospels, is a crucial period in Christianity marking the events leading up to Jesus Christ's crucifixion, death, and resurrection. It includes key events such as Jesus' triumphal entry into Jerusalem, the Last Supper with his disciples on Wednesday, his crucifixion later that afternoon, and his resurrection on Sunday dawn.

Identifying and verifying the correct observance of the Sabbath following the crucifixion is important for many Christian denominations and traditions. This day holds deep theological and spiritual significance. Was it the day symbolizing the rest and renewal that comes after the sacrifice of Good Friday and leading into the celebration of Easter Sunday, which represents hope, rebirth, and redemption for believers? It wasn't Saturday, on which the weekly Sabbath was observed as we have discussed earlier.

And so, while all days may be considered equal and good in a general sense, there are certain times and events that hold specific significance in religious and spiritual practices. By recognizing these sacred days, individuals can deepen their connection to their faith, find strength and inspiration in communal worship, and reaffirm their spiritual beliefs in a meaningful way.

Revisiting the Timeline of Jesus' Crucifixion and Resurrection.

The traditional association of Jesus' crucifixion with Good Friday requires correction. A closer examination of the biblical account reveals a different sequence of events.

Tuesday, 13th Abib/Nissan AD 27, was the day of preparation for Passover. During the day, Jesus' disciples prepared the Upper Room for the impending feast. That evening, as the 14th Abib began, Jesus and His disciples shared the Last Supper and inaugurated the first Lord's Communion Service.

The next morning, Wednesday, 14th Abib, Jesus faced trial and was crucified in the afternoon. The following day, Thursday, 15th Abib, was the High Sabbath, as ordained in Exodus 16:16.

Friday, 16th Abib, was a regular day, allowing the women to prepare spices and ointments for Jesus' tomb. According to custom, they would visit the tomb before sunrise.

Saturday, 17th Abib, marked the weekly Sabbath, instituted by the Manna Sabbath in Exodus 16:25-26.

Finally, on Sunday, 18th Abib, the first day of the week, the women approached the tomb at dawn, bearing spices and ointments. To their astonishment, they discovered Jesus had risen, fulfilling His promise of three days and three nights in the tomb.

This revised timeline clarifies the events surrounding Jesus' crucifixion and resurrection, aligning with biblical accounts and historical accuracy.

Key dates:
- Tuesday, 13th Abib: Day of preparation
- Wednesday, 14th Abib: Last Supper, trial, and crucifixion
- Thursday, 15th Abib: High Sabbath
- Friday, 16th Abib: Women prepare spices and ointments
- Saturday, 17th Abib: Weekly Sabbath
- Sunday, 18th Abib: Jesus' resurrection

In conclusion, the week has two highly significant days - the Seventh Day for the Old Testament and the first day of the week in the New Testament.

The Seventh Day, or the Sabbath, was central to the Promised Land. The Bible instructs that if you honor your father and mother, your days will be prolonged in the land that the Lord gives you (Exodus 20:12, Deuteronomy 5:16).

Equally important is the first day of the week, commonly known as the Lord's Day, which commemorates Jesus' resurrection, believed to have occurred at or before dawn on Sunday.

These two pivotal days parallel the first day of creation, in which God created light - the first of all his creations. Nothing else was made on that day, yet this light was invisible but enabled visibility, inaccessible, immortal, infinite, and everlasting.

The seventh day of creation is another parallel, in which God rested from the literal act of creation. However, this "resting" was not due to tiredness, but rather the creation of rest, relaxation, meditation, joy, adoration, hallowing, and all the virtues that provide comfort, rejuvenation, and refocus for humanity.

This interconnectedness underscores the continuity between creation, covenant, and redemption, highlighting the significance of these two days in the biblical narrative.

Jesus Christ, the beginning and the end, the first and the last, the alpha and the omega, encapsulates the essence of creation. As the firstborn of all creation, He is both the source and culmination of everything.

The creation narrative illustrates this parallel, where the first day, marked by Light, was replicated six times, leading to the seventh day. This underscores Jesus' fundamental role: without the initial Light, no subsequent days could exist.

John 1:3 confirms this, attributing all creation to Him. Jesus Christ possesses absolute authority, unlocking and locking with sovereign power. He is God's wisdom incarnate, representing both creation's beginning and ultimate fulfillment in the Sabbath.

The convergence of Jewish and Christian worship practices on separate days – Saturday for some, Sunday for others – is not a coincidence or divergence, but a reflection of shared roots and distinct perspectives.

Both days hold significance, yet each community assigns unique importance to their chosen day of worship. The Book of Revelation mentions 12,000 individuals from each of Israel's 12 tribes, destined for a special place in God's Kingdom (Revelation 7:4-8). Notably, the Bible doesn't imply these individuals are exclusively Christian.

Christianity emphasizes that sainthood transcends ethnicity and gender, recognizing only faith in Christ and adherence to His teachings (Galatians 3:26-28, Romans 2:28-29).

It's possible that some Jewish individuals may find salvation through their Sabbath observance, known only to God. The New Testament affirms that all days are equally sacred (Romans 14:5-6, Galatians 4:9-10), suggesting that the Lord's Day and Sabbath serve as spiritual catalysts, inspiring devotion and faith in those who observe them.

In this sense, the distinction between Saturday and Sunday becomes secondary to the shared pursuit of spiritual connection and reverence for God.

Both days facilitate an encounter with the divine, nurturing faith and community among believers.

This nuanced understanding acknowledges the complexity of Jewish-Christian relations, highlighting the complementary nature of their worship traditions rather than perpetuating divisions.

Jesus Christ is the head of the universal, invisible church, encompassing all saints from Adam and Eve to the present. This diverse community includes those who observed the Sabbath and those who didn't, as well as those who died before reaching the Promised Land.

Despite their differences, all these saints will collectively enter Jesus Christ's rest – the ultimate Sabbath – as promised in Scripture. The Bible emphasizes that salvation comes solely through faith in God's only begotten Son, Jesus Christ (John 3:16, Acts 4:12), rather than observance of specific days.

In other words, salvation is not contingent upon keeping the Sabbath or any other day, but rather on believing in Jesus Christ. His sacrifice transcends temporal boundaries, uniting saints across time and space.

As Hebrews 4:9-10 affirms, believers will enter God's rest, where "there remains, then, a Sabbath-rest for the people of God." This eternal rest supersedes earthly observances, welcoming all who trust in Jesus Christ, regardless of their historical or cultural context.

Through faith in Christ, the saints of all ages will experience the ultimate fulfillment of God's promise of rest, unity, and eternal life.

The Israelites, God's chosen people, constituted a physical nation, foreshadowing the spiritual nation of the Church. Consequently, God's covenant with them emphasized physical rewards, such as the Promised Land of Canaan, rather than eternal life.

The Israelites' experience illustrates this distinction. Of those who left Egypt and reached adulthood, only Joshua and Caleb entered the Promised Land. Nonetheless, even their clothing, including shoes, and Joseph's 300-year-old remains did reach Canaan. This outcome wasn't total failure, as the promise was physical and subject to mortality.

In the Old Testament, disobedience regarding Sabbath observance resulted in physical punishment or exclusion from Israel, but not spiritual death. In contrast, the New Testament establishes a spiritual covenant between God and humanity, with eternal consequences.

Notably, failing to observe the Sabbath, a physical requirement in the Old Testament, doesn't exclude one from Christianity. However, gathering in God's presence revitalizes the spirit, while neglecting communal worship can lead to spiritual stagnation.

This highlights the shift from physical to spiritual focus in the New Testament. While physical obedience was crucial in the Old Covenant, spiritual faithfulness defines the New Covenant. Gathering to worship and honor God nourishes believers' spiritual lives, regardless of the day or specific observance.

In essence, the Israelites' physical experience prefigured the spiritual reality fulfilled in Jesus Christ, emphasizing the distinction between physical and spiritual covenants, rewards, and consequences.

As physical beings, we're influenced by our surroundings, including atmospheric conditions, celestial bodies, and cosmic forces. To thrive, we should heed the commandments given to Israel, originally intended for their physical well-being.

God's instructions regarding days, dates, seasons, locations, and other aspects of life benefit humanity, not Himself. While some divine principles remain mysteries, our role is to obey His commandments, trusting in His wisdom, as expressed in Deuteronomy 29:29.

In the Passion Week context, understanding the biblical calendar sheds light on crucial events. Specifically, the first Sabbath of the Feast of Unleavened Bread precedes Good Friday, and the weekly Sabbath follows Good Friday.

Good Friday is flanked by two Sabbaths: the 15th of Abib, the first day of Unleavened Bread, and the 21st of Abib, the seventh day. These biblical events mark the first recorded Holy Convocations, or high day Sabbaths, occurring on the first and seventh days of the Unleavened Bread week. Significantly, they prefigure the Passion week, where Passover reached its climax in the Last Supper and crucifixion of Jesus Christ, the Lamb of God.

In this prophetic parallel, the Unleavened Bread week's beginning and ending Sabbaths foreshadowed the pivotal moments of Christ's passion. The initial Sabbath inaugurated the week-long celebration, while the final Sabbath brought closure, symbolizing the ultimate rest and redemption achieved through Jesus' sacrifice.

These dates correspond to the first Sabbaths mentioned following the very first Passover in 1435 BCE.

These events foreshadowed the Last Supper and Jesus Christ's crucifixion on the 14th of Abib in 27 AD. Recognizing these connections deepens our understanding of God's redemptive plan and the significance of biblical observances.

By embracing God's commandments and acknowledging the mysteries beyond our comprehension, we align ourselves with His divine purpose, honoring the intricate interplay between physical and spiritual realities.

In this context, "Beyond Good Friday," there are two separate and distinct Sabbaths: the first day of the Feast of Unleavened Bread, which precedes it and marks the beginning of the week-long celebration, and the weekly Sabbath, which follows it and falls at the end of the week.

These two Sabbaths are distinct in purpose and significance: one commemorates the start of the Unleavened Bread Feast, while the other observes the weekly rest and worship.

This sequence highlights the unique convergence of sacred days in the Passion Week narrative, underscoring the connection between Passover, Unleavened Bread, and the resurrection of Jesus Christ.

About the Author

Jaison Ndlovu, born on July 1, 1960, in Guruve, Zimbabwe, grew up in Bharamasvesve, Zhombe, Kwekwe. He is the second child and eldest son of Katazo Amos Magundwane and Resiya Chikwinya. With four sisters and four brothers, he attended Gwesela St Andrew's School, St Martin de Porres, and Ascot Secondary School for his education. He pursued salesmanship at the Union College of South Africa and Religious Studies at Ambassador Bible College. Jaison is married to Susan Ndlovu (nee Mahogo), and they have four sons and two daughters, all of whom are married. Staying at Empress in Zhombe, Zimbabwe, he is an active contributor as a blogger and editor on Wikipedia, and shares video songs and sermons on YouTube.